Reclaiming
Quiet

Reclaiming Quiet

Cultivating a Life of Holy Attention

SARAH CLARKSON

BakerBooks

a division of Baker Publishing Group
Grand Rapids, Michigan

© 2024 by Sarah Clarkson

Published by Baker Books
a division of Baker Publishing Group
Grand Rapids, Michigan
BakerBooks.com

Printed in the United States of America

Library of Congress Cataloging-in-Publication Data
Names: Clarkson, Sarah (Editor for Whole Heart Press), author.
Title: Reclaiming quiet : cultivating a life of Holy attention / Sarah Clarkson.
Description: Grand Rapids, Michigan : Baker Books, a division of Baker Publishing Group, [2024] | Includes bibliographical references.
Identifiers: LCCN 2024005425 | ISBN 9781540900524 (paper) | ISBN 9781540903198 (casebound) | ISBN 9781493439515 (ebook)
Subjects: LCSH: Quietude—Moral and ethical aspects. | Quietude—Religious aspects.
Classification: LCC BJ1533.Q5 C433 2024 | DDC 128/.4—dc23/eng/20240429
LC record available at https://lccn.loc.gov/2024005425

Unless otherwise indicated, Scripture quotations are from the (NASB®) New American Standard Bible®. Copyright © 1960, 1971, 1977, 1995 by The Lockman Foundation. Used by permission. All rights reserved. www.lockman.org

Scripture quotations labeled ESV are from The Holy Bible, English Standard Version® (ESV®). Copyright © 2001 by Crossway, a publishing ministry of Good News Publishers. Used by permission. All rights reserved. ESV Text Edition: 2016

Scripture quotations labeled KJV are from the King James Version of the Bible.

Cover art: abstract painting *Promise* © by Stephanie Marzella

Published in association with The Bindery Agency, www.TheBinderyAgency.com

Baker Publishing Group publications use paper produced from sustainable forestry practices and postconsumer waste whenever possible.

24 25 26 27 28 29 30   7 6 5 4 3

To my children, for whose sake I have sought the quiet,
in whose presence I have gleaned its wonder.

Contents

Introduction

Kingfisher Sight

"If you keep your eyes out, you might see a kingfisher. I saw one down by the lake the other day," Mark said.

The words of our new friend startled me. Kingfishers? I'd yearned for years to witness one of these magical birds; they haunt the lines of countless poems I love, dashes of electric blue whose presence is like the flash of divinity. Swift and small, they always seem to appear in books as portents of some subtle revelation or gift. Mark's words reached my ears on one of our first Sundays in the church to which my husband, Thomas, had come as priest. The world and ways of our parish were still new to us, each day an exploration. We'd begun to fill and form the great rooms of our old Victorian vicarage. We'd found the bridge over the lake that led to the woods. We'd met the ducks and chased the trains down the nearby track and visited the farmers' market down the lane. But kingfishers, my goodness, this was a grace beyond expectation.

"Where did you see it?" I asked a little breathlessly. Mark, whose knowledge of the natural world and our little neighborhood were a constant gift, described the spot in detail and added that he'd actually seen three. "But you have to be in a certain state of heart," he warned. "And then, you just see them."

Ah, yes.

Of course. I knew in an instant what he meant. If there was one thing I had pondered in the years before our move to this new home, it was just this: how to dwell in the kind of quiet that opens one up to the gift and wonder of the world.

Quiet has been my study, my pursuit—my frustration, even— for most of the last three years. Mark's comment about the state of heart needed to spot a kingfisher sums up in an image what I mean by *quiet*: an openness to the presence of God at play in creation, at work in our hearts, directing our ways and drawing us into his story. I suppose that's a lot to pile on the shoulders of quiet as a concept. But after all these years of study and pursuit, I am convinced that our capacity to be quiet will shape the whole of the way we come to love and trust the living God, to have a lively faith at all.

I started this journey deeper into the realms of quiet (for journey it is; I'm nowhere near its end) because I was exhausted. We'd come to the end of the first pandemic year; I found my-self expecting a third child after a season of illness and felt the severe isolation of a new lockdown to be almost unbearable. I could not get my hands round peace, and my mind felt in a constant state of uproar. On New Year's Day, I read Psalm 23 and those words—"he leads me beside quiet waters, he restores my soul"—became the theme and cadence of my prayer as we entered the new year and the coming of our child.

But I quickly realized my prayer was not one God would answer with a sudden dump of serenity. As I prayed almost desperately for peace, I began to be aware of the patterns and shapes of daily life by which I was driving a certain frenzy within myself, by which I was disquieting my own mind. Every day I crammed it with the images and thoughts of countless screens and headlines. I turned compulsively to my phone not only in moments of relaxation but also in anxiety. I began to wonder if at times my smartphone had become my replacement for the Holy Spirit, the ever-present comforter I turned to in times of fear. I noticed the heightened stress I felt, the phantom fear of being left out because the online world was always updating. I realized how much I had become driven as a writer by a need to produce work that was rooted not in conviction or joy but in the restless competition stoked by the online world.

And all these habits were shaping my outer life, drawing the hours of my rest or work into their whirlwind, invading the moments of my outdoor wandering, my mothering and rest, my daily capacity to walk in joy. I wanted God to give me quiet and bring me rest, but all the habits of my daily existence were shaping a life of exhaustion, of inward disquiet and outward unease.

I don't think I'm alone in this. I think that we in the modern world increasingly struggle to hear the voice of God, and sometimes we forget to even desire it because our minds and ears are so crammed with the voices online of the internet, headlines, social media, and news feeds. Our attention is drawn constantly to the addictive scroll of a feed or screen, our minds trained to skim information, restless for the next tidbit, incapable of rest or depth. Our devices are with us at all times so that whether we walk, rest, grieve, work, or sleep, we never need to be silent.

But I believe our greatest loss is spiritual because our *disquiet* leads us to a certain kind of life; it shapes the whole of the way we interact with each other and the world around us. We become driven by a sense of urgency, stressed and distracted from the moment we wake to the moment we sleep. We become increasingly disconnected from our physical and emotional surroundings, incapable of enjoying a nature walk without a screen to document it, increasingly dismissive of the tiny and faithful acts of the ordinary that constitute the spiritual richness or poverty of our everyday lives. Our inner worlds are so noisy with the countless images we have seen that there is no room for worship, rest, or real and heart-changing prayer.

What, then, shall we do?

God's answer to my desperate prayer three years ago was to invite me to journey homeward, into the realm of quiet where rest always waits and love always gleams. God does not change. His grace is not dependent upon how disciplined we are or how good we've been, but sometimes the grace we most need to experience is his aid in healing the forms of life that have made him feel distant to us. This book is my invitation to you as a reader to journey with me, to journey homeward to a life and heart rooted in a peace beyond the touch of any trouble in this world.

We are called to quiet, all of us; this is what I have come to believe with the whole of my heart. Every Christian is called to cultivate kingfisher sight, to a life shaped not by a frenzied mind or a changing screen but by a heart set fast upon the light of our Maker as his love invades our hearts and all the world.

Too often, though, we hear the word *quiet* as something negative and abstract, a subtraction of activity or even a relationship available only to mystics and saints. Too often we think of it as merely a discipline we cannot manage, another hard thing that only the very holy or very rigid can attain. But every Christian is called to be a person capable of hearing the voice of the Holy Spirit, of practicing God's presence in the midst of the everyday. Quiet is not a special state reserved for introverts or particularly pious people or the lonely. Every Christian is called to cultivate an interior world, to make mind and heart a space of expectant silence as we wait for God to speak his Word into our darkness and sing us back to life. Quiet is the space from which we pray and worship, the condition of our learning, our creativity, our literal "in" sight.

In this book, I want to explore what it looks like for an ordinary person to choose the radical way of quiet. To slowly (and often with great difficulty) choose the patterns and ways of hush rather than of hurry or information. To open days with prayer or a moment of stillness instead of a quick scroll on a screen. To turn, in grief or fear, to the inner refuge of God's presence rather than Google.

This book is written as much out of my frailty as my strength. This is a work of exploration, sometimes exasperation, and, just now and then, epiphany.

I struggle with addiction to my phone. I wrestle with boredom in prayer. My work here proceeds from my life as a writer (working intensively online), as a mother of four adorable and very active children, and as a vicar's wife with the social schedule this entails. I am a soul seeking to take part in the issues of my generation yet deeply convicted that I am called to cultivate a life shaped by the holy wild of quiet so that God's Word may sing amidst my days.

I love the contemplatives, the saints of heroic prayer and vast silences, but this is not a book about the contemplative life. It's not an exploration of radical acts or extreme states. The thing is, I don't think quiet is really about great feats so much as it is about small faithfulnesses. And that's a work available to every believer alive.

What I am asking is how we may grow quiet in our lives again like a seed planted in the ground. It may burgeon into a great tree that gives form to the whole shape of our living in the world—it may bear contemplative, radical fruit. But here in the rush and flow of daily need and demand, how may we cradle and tend the seed of quiet in our hearts so that something new begins to grow in the fallow earth of our hurry and fear and distraction?

I did see a kingfisher eventually, you know.

A dash of the brightest blue I've ever seen, a flash of grace amidst the scratch of wintry branches and rush of brown river water as I walked home down the footpath one day.

It must have been at least six months after my talk with Mark. By that time, I'd forgotten to look, had ceased a kind of inward striving toward attention. My life was just as busy, my sight still more entangled than I liked with screens, my days full with need and demand. The only difference I could see in myself was just . . . the opening of my hands. I'd managed that a little more in those months. The opening of my heart here and there throughout the day to listen for the windsong of God's presence, the news of his weather, his goodness at work within the wildlands of my heart. I'd honored my limits a bit more, too, learned to assent to the smallness of my days and the smallness of my strength.

And there it was, my little flash of blue quiet, of sapphire peace, a sign of the love always haunting my steps.

As it does yours.

May you find that same love drawing your own heart into the great quiet of God's presence in the pages that follow.

Sarah Clarkson
The Vicarage, Oxford
2023

Part One

The Nature of Quiet

1

Kitchen Table in My Heart

Presence

The priest, my friend, set a cup of coffee before me. A brown pottery cup and saucer brimming with black, fragrant liquid. The morning light slanted in through the tall kitchen windows, silvered September rays that rippled over my hands. Time slowed. I rested my hands on the gold-grained wood of the table and watched the steam rise from the cup. The echo and thrum of cars in the street sounded faintly in the bright room. A strip of blue sky sliced through the London rooftops, and I watched a bird leap from ledge to ledge in joyous bursts of flight. I cradled the cup in my hands and took a sip. But for a long moment I could not take another, for I knew that if I did, I might begin to cry.

The morning had not started with any intimation of emotional crisis. The kitchen in which I sat was part of the vicarage belonging to the old East London church next door. My husband, Thomas, training for ordination in the Church of

England, was doing a placement at the church. Our hosts were the resident priest and his wife, old friends of ours from Oxford who had invited us and our six-month-old daughter to live with them for the monthlong duration of Thomas's stay. We had arrived perhaps a little crazy-eyed. The passionate weariness and joy of our first months as new parents lay just behind us (along with my husband's eight final exams), as did my own release of a book with all the invasive online work such things require. I had no real expectations for that month other than the care of our daughter and a little prowling about the London streets. I knew myself to be a little exhausted, a little lonely, a little fragmented by the online world, but I had not yet faced the huge ache gathering in the inmost spaces of my heart.

That morning began as many did in that season; I wrestled with my babe after her nap, trying, with frustrated clumsiness, to feed her some oatmeal. Her resistant squawks echoed down the hallway, and when my priest friend came into the kitchen after the morning service, I hastily gathered our things to try to get us mercifully out of his way. The nuisance of us invading the calm working space of his kitchen table on a busy morning must have, I felt, stretched even the kindliest of friendships.

But, "No!" he said. "Stay, please, you're no bother. Would you like some coffee? I think I'll make some coffee."

I could not lie. I greatly desired coffee and so nodded my head, expecting a hasty mug, for I knew his morning was full with local demands. But he sat me back at the table. He gave my baby a spoon to play with and began to chat quietly with me about all sorts of strange and wondrous things as he put the kettle on to boil, moving gently about the kitchen in his cassock. Liturgies and honeybees, and the joys of rooftop gardens. He gave me an old hand-worked coffee grinder and told me to turn

18

it while he got the cups. Its crunch and whir were immensely satisfying, the scent of the fresh coffee like tonic to my weary awareness as I opened the drawer and tipped it into a bowl for him to use. He brewed the coffee in a brown ceramic jug and got us out a set of earthenware cups and saucers. He poured the coffee strong and set my cup and saucer before me. I expected him to then move swiftly away, but instead he pulled out a chair and sat companionably with me in a great and gentle quiet.

That quiet; it was a living, benevolent thing, and in its presence, I felt myself waken, felt my skin and senses sharpen, felt something like grief stir in the deep places of my heart, a yearning that had not wakened in me for many days. I hungered for quiet, not just the cessation of noise but that deep inward hush in which the kindness of God is the light burning at the back of our eyes so that we look upon the world in the brightness of his companionship. For many months, I had not been able to find or conjure that quiet in myself. The wind breathed in now through the high windows. A bird called in the courtyard below. The coffee burned wonderfully in my throat, and that is when I knew I might cry.

For in the gift of that drink and the kindly presence attending it, I knew two things viscerally and at once:

I was riven with homesickness for a larger quiet.

I was already cradled by the very thing I thought that homecoming would bring me: the kindly presence of my God.

———

I first knew quiet as if it were a realm within my mind. A secret place that was my fortress, my lookout upon the busy world. In quiet I reigned, peering out upon my surroundings with the clarity and attention that is its gift.

I think most children are born with this hush that is a kind of contemplation. Children watch. They listen. They take in everything around them in a way almost terrifying. Quiet, for a child, is native, and in that sense, I barely remember it. I only remember the intensity of the world's beauty, the way an autumn leaf or a cloud could speak to me as if with an audible voice. I remember the way I could gather myself into myself, draw all my powers inward to some interior room where I could imagine or wonder, where I could rest. I remember the depth of my feeling, the true and urgent dramas of childhood grief and love that are the soul's first encounters with the oceanic forces of human feeling. The potency of the world is something children apprehend in a powerful way, a sense well blunted in us as adults.

It's something we can recover, a faculty we may hone.

But quiet is not primarily a practice; it is a homeland, one as instinctive to me in adulthood as it was in my innocence. I can still remember the sense of a unity within myself, an inward rest, a space of almost physically located hush to which I could return each night. And while I dove, as every child does, into all the action and drama of the world—friendship and study, play and creativity, first loves and deep losses—that quiet inward place remained.

But quiet was also the companion of my grief.

Perhaps it was amidst disaster that I first began to understand the true nature of quiet. I was seventeen when mental illness invaded and shattered my mind. Then there was a great, gaping silence. The quiet of that season was terrible at first, attended always by fear and the horrific, intrusive images brought on by my illness (OCD). I thought, at first, that I had lost both God and quiet itself to the violence of what filled my broken mind.

But as the months passed and I learned to live in the company of horror, I began to realize that the horror did not reach or alter that deep presence of quiet within me. Silence now stretched long around me; I was eighteen, incapable of moving out or taking up the adult life for which I yearned. I spent hours alone in my room, grieved and yearning.

But in that wasteland of my heart, I found the ancient, gracious quiet of my childhood still waiting.

Of course, in those days I didn't have a Facebook account. I didn't have a laptop or a mobile phone. When I withdrew into my room, depressed and despairing, to wrestle with loss and horror and disappointment, I had little to distract me. The quiet at first seemed just empty. But soon it became a place I could dwell where a presence—something kind and gentle that was not threatened by the bleak horizons of my broken mind—waited to comfort me. I took long walks in the mountains and spent aching hours alone with my Bible, a journal, or a book. Those were agonizing years in which I watched every good I expected, every adventure I yearned to accomplish, move just beyond my grasp.

But they were also years of discovery. I began a great season of reading prompted by my forced purchase of St. Teresa of Ávila's *Interior Castle* after I accidentally spilled coffee on its pages in a bookstore and found a description of the soul as a castle where the Beloved dwells. I began to read voraciously; it was my consolation and escape from the darkness, and through it I discovered other authors who had walked the road of quiet. Those bitter years of hushed, hungry reading became the ground of my adult faith. I learned to truly expect God's arrival in the vast silence of my need, for as Brother Lawrence (a seventeenth-century monk who sought God's presence in

21

the most mundane of tasks) wrote, "He is nearer to us than we think."[1] I learned to let prayer shape the way I saw the world, to "behold the lightener of the stars"[2] as the Celtic Christians did in their ancient prayers, and to understand that the Creator's breath blew also in the dark and void places of my heart.

Those writers, those saints, taught me to seek a listening heart as the fundamental orientation of a Christian, one who is literally redeemed by the Word made flesh of a speaking God who fills our silence with his voice. When I discovered Hans Urs von Balthasar (the great twentieth-century theologian who constructed his systematic theology around truth, goodness, and beauty) and read his commentary on Irenaeus, I was struck and awed by his idea that when God pours out his Holy Spirit within us, we are entrusted with the most intimate thoughts and speech of God himself.

For about a dozen years, I read and hungered and learned. I lived within the harsh confines of anxiety. Leaving home, spending even the night away from family, left me in the clutches of black, breathless panic attacks. But those years saw my slow journey to an adult life and a faith that could contain both my illness and my hope. I began to climb out of the crater in which mental illness placed me to find a manageable place in a world I now knew was almost unbearably broken but also shot through with the presence of a Healer. I emerged out of that season into an overseas move, into student life at thirty years old, then (to my startled, unraveled gratitude) marriage and motherhood. But ever amidst these growing gifts, the great comfort of my journeying, the secret treasure of my days, was the quiet I held as a holy, wild, and precious thing, the native place within my heart to which I could return and find a Lover waiting.

Until I lost the way to that homeland.

I don't know when it began, exactly. Perhaps it was when I got my first smartphone and was unaware of the way it slipped into the spaces that used to be sacred to a gathered hush, the moments of solitude when I might look long out the window of either my eyes or my soul. Maybe it was when my mind leapt onto the track of academic push and deadline. Perhaps it came with the larger need and exhaustion of parenthood. Perhaps I became disoriented by the grieved, restless anxiety of a news cycle I could always refresh and could not look away from. All that loneliness and fear, the unrest of a grieving world, perhaps those were the storms that broke my tether to the hushed trust of quiet.

Somewhere along the way, my mind became crowded with the images and thoughts of countless screens and headlines, my soul restless and on edge, and the way to quiet, even in solitude, was no longer plain to me. I watched myself become increasingly formed and driven by my inward distraction, my incapacity to be still, my unease with hush. I witnessed the holy quiet of those early years being swallowed by the buzz of a mind primed to turn to a screen for comfort, addicted to headlines. I felt chased by all I witnessed online and all I must accomplish, desperate both to keep up with and also attend to the myriad voices calling out in sorrow or anger or outrage in the words on my screen. I could no longer look away from them without a mighty inward wrestle, and even then, I was haunted by the echoes of their frenzy and fury. And in that haunting, I knew myself lost and wandering, far from the homeland of my heart.

I just didn't know how far I'd gotten until I tasted an almost unbearable grace that autumn day at the vicarage kitchen table.

St. Teresa discovered a palace within her soul.

I found a kitchen table in mine.

Both were hallowed and wondrous because of the God who waited to laugh and talk with us both in those inmost spaces of our hearts.

Somewhere between the catch of my breath and the next sip of coffee at the vicarage table that morning, my breath began to slow. Sometimes an act of kindness can create a moment of blessed disruption, a suspended space that allows us to step out of a headlong rush in a certain direction. That month in London, away from the normal patterns of our intense lives in that season, allowed me that radical step out of my inner frenzy. I let my inward clamor die away day by day and tried, with an effort born of deep desire, to leave the furor of my screens and attend instead to the quiet spaces of that London home, to the East End streets in their weave toward the Thames, to the face of my baby, still so new to me and so eager to reveal a thousand daily secrets.

I stepped back into a sense of God's companionship.

That was, perhaps, the greatest gift of the priest's kindness to me. In the generosity of his own peaceful presence, I found that God had not, as I thought, withdrawn from me in frustration. He was still there, gracious as my friend, fragrant as the coffee, tender as the autumn light, and in the revelatory brightness of those graces, I remembered afresh that his presence is constant, never dependent upon my discipline. He waits, always he waits, to receive us in that inmost room, and day by day I knew that again as I had known it in the early days of my illness when it was the shelter that kept me in life.

But the shape of our lives in that house allowed me to inhabit that knowledge in a radical way. I began to remember there is a physical shape, a rhythm to the cultivation of quiet. The act of my priest friend that day, his decision to set aside all the clamoring details in order to make me coffee, to savor the quiet with me, was an act rooted in a larger pattern of living. A pattern, first, of prayer; day and night my friend said the services of morning and evening prayer and offered a simple eucharistic service. The whole of our lives that season revolved around those times. Even when I (usually) couldn't attend, I watched Thomas go and heard the hum of voices echoing up into the old kitchen where I sat with my daughter and opened my own heart to God.

Our lives there were patterned, too, on rest. There was a spaciousness to time there I had not experienced for a good long while. We didn't hurry, and that felt astonishing. Just as prayer could not be rushed, so each conversation, each meal, each morning and evening were too precious to be worried along to an early close. There was time amidst the demands of parish life for our friends to make fresh bread many days, bread we slathered with honey culled from the bees they kept on the vicarage rooftop. Many evenings we lingered in the kitchen for hours with little candles lit as we drank the good red wine our friends had gotten on holiday and shared with us freely. Some nights we sat by the fire as the days grew darker and the air grew chill. I felt, as I moved through those days, that I was learning how to walk again, how to move without hurry, how to look without distraction.

The kitchen was my special refuge. It became the place of my homecoming to quiet. I sat there often during the day, resting in the great, window-lit silence. I drank Dorset tea in a blue and white china mug. I reveled in the warmth of the air in the kitchen, the gentle glow of heat kept alight by the faithful old mint-green Aga that sat in the corner. It became the "outward and visible sign" of the grace I was recovering in my heart.

An Aga is an old-fashioned cooker (range) with two hobs (burners) always at low heat (they have covers) and two ovens beneath. An Aga can heat a whole house, and they conjure an almost enchanted comfort around themselves. I'd read about them before in English novels, and the way they're described makes them sound almost mythical, like little household goddesses: potent, symbolic shapes of hearthside comfort. They suggest not just that elemental good of warmth in winter but also strong tea brewed in brown pots, fresh baking, and the gathering of friends. The Aga in my friend's kitchen was a benevolent old queen of radiant warmth that eased me every time I entered her presence.

And with her warmth came a blessed slowness, the sense of things made not on the instant but with the kind of gentle, attentive movement that is a dance made to the teakettle and kitchen sink music of the ordinary. The sort of music that turns one's eyes back to the window, coaxes one into a chair, and leaves one simply watching. And the quiet I found was like that kindly Aga, making a gentle, radiant space in which I could sit down and speak with the Beloved.

In the story of the world's ending told in Revelation, we find that in the world to come—the sweet world that will last unblemished, ungrieved—no light is needed because God himself will be our light. It's hard to imagine what it means to live in the presence of a light that is itself, himself, our Maker, to see and love and breathe in the gentle brightness of God. But it is a life, I believe, we begin to imagine here in a world still haunted by darkness, begin to live because the light whose love will irradiate eternity dwells now within our hearts.

What is quiet but basking in that given and kindly light?

What is quiet but resting in the brightness whose presence within our hearts remakes the world?

What is our work when it comes to the keeping of quiet but a return to the grace and brightness, the kitchen table company of the God whose gracious presence in the inmost rooms of our hearts invites us even now to stand in the all-suffusing light of eternity?

But how?

As I've wrestled through this book on quiet, I've also worked my way a page a day through a writing of the early church, *On the Incarnation*. In its closing pages, after a crescendo of an ending to a theological treatise written to praise the matchless things God has done to heal and save humanity and free us from death, the great church father Athanasius concludes rather pragmatically by urging his readers to "the good life and a pure soul and virtue." For, he says, "without a pure mind and a life modeled on the saints, no one can understand the words of the saints."[3] I think what he means by that is close to what Jesus said to a seeker who wanted to know if he was truly the Messiah: if anyone desires to know the truth about Jesus's words, he has only to obey them in order to discover the grace and truth they bring.

I've thought often about Athanasius's sudden transposition here, his abrupt move from pages and pages of visionary description about the glories of the incarnation, with its worldwide implications for battles ended and devils thrown down and barbarians tamed, to a rather workaday insistence on practical virtue. We must not merely study these ideas, it seems, but rather embody them. This is the only way we may come both to understand

and, more vitally, to inhabit the divine work of the incarnation as it tethers us afresh to the life of God. Our action comes, in a radical and roundabout way, before our full understanding. We have to live in such a way that knowledge ripens in body as well as mind, in affection as well as soul, as we mold our lives by eternal rhythms and shapes rather than those of a fallen world.

This, I believe, is what it means to choose and live by quiet.

I think this is the work I stumbled back into at my friend's kitchen table, one I have chosen to pursue, however imperfectly, every day since. We are asked to shape our lives, our time, our attention by habits and rhythms radically different from the windblown fury of the broken world. This means an entirely alternate shape of life, not just the subtraction of screens and distractions but the embrace of prayer, of daily wonder, of listening, of trust, of celebration that roots us moment by moment in that deep, watchful quiet that ushers us into the presence of God.

I still own a smartphone. I live in the modern world. But I am walking ancient paths in learning the rhythms, the habits, the steps and cadence by which I may root not just my mind but my body, my wearied senses, and my breath in the homeland of quiet.

As I write, the pale, luminous light of a later winter afternoon in England pours in through the southern windows of my study and falls upon my hands. These hands creased with age and work, this tired skin that yet contains the thrum of my human soul, this body and these eyes watching that riverlike light, this frail self of mine mired in a fallen world, invited into the light of my Maker. I lift my hands from the keyboard. They are suffused in a brightness so gentle I could weep. I close my eyes, filled within myself by the radiance that is the quiet, world-healing presence of my Maker.

I sit down at the table he has set within my heart.

Pray

O God, who waits to greet us within the castles and kitch-ens of our hearts, draw us to the hearthside of your pres-ence. Send silence to halt our frenzied ways and quiet to lead us homeward to where your love has laid a feast. Help us to recall the grace in which we already stand, the love that need never be asked for because it is already given, the home that has already been made in our hearts by your Spirit and waits for our weary arrival. Teach us to trust the hope that quiet kindles and walk in its healing ways until we find the homeward road, through Jesus Christ our Lord, Amen.

Ponder

- What sort of room do you imagine at the center of your heart? Kitchen, front porch, banquet hall? Allow your-self to picture that space and imagine God sitting at the heart of it, ready to speak with you.
- When was the last time you had a deep sense of quiet? What were the conditions, the graces, the circumstances that made it possible?
- Consider: Is quiet something you miss? If so, why? And what influence or presence makes it most difficult to find?

2

Native Ground

Home

When I was a child, I lived in the hill country of rural Texas beyond the reach of any nighttime light but the stars. When darkness fell it was absolute. Sometimes in winter, when evening came early and our parents talked for hours inside, my friends and I would foray into that vast, rural blackness for a game of hide-and-seek. We always stayed near the house at first, in the lit portions of the yard. The house lights made great yellow circles that felt like the watchtowers of a fortress, shielding us from the night beyond. But always, always I felt myself tugged into the oceanic black that lapped on the edges of home light, drawn by the presence of something I couldn't quantify or contain. It took me a while, but eventually I'd slip out the garden gate, beyond the farthest reach of the light, and crouch beside the fence, unbearably curious at what waited in the shadows beyond. The fields ebbed away from me into a darkness so vast and long it took me a few minutes to get brave enough to face it. I'd sit there, letting my sight, my hearing, my skin adjust to the absolute dark as it crept up behind me. I felt very small. And often, at first, wildly afraid.

Quiet often feels that way to me at first, a vast presence that is my fascination and also my dread.

These days, the vast, rural nights of my childhood have given way to the sky I can glimpse out my bedroom window in England. My chair is pulled close to the panes so I can watch that sky through the toss of tree branches and the flicker of leaves. When I first saw the bedroom in the old English vicarage that would belong to me, I imagined it would make me capable of the hushed discipline for which I yearned. With such a window—a wall of a window, paned in hundred-year-old glass, with the dappled sheen of a lake beyond and those great, guardian trees—I could focus. I could listen. I could pray.

But the darkness that grew each evening in the panes brought with it a touch of my childhood terror, the sense of awed dread I'd felt in the Texas countryside. I came to it in such exhaustion after our move, after the days of settling our small children into a new life. I began to sit by that window just as winter slipped into the world, darkening the sky at four o'clock, chilling the panes. I sat in silence, and it was . . . void. Cold. All that echoed in it seemed to be the erratic breath of my great weariness.

Quiet, even when chosen, can feel at first like darkness. I sit down to be silent and know I've entered a vast space whose borders I cannot see, whose paths I cannot navigate or trace. Sometimes, when I push away the great cacophony of noise and screen and distraction, the first thing I feel is a kind of abandonment. At that moment, the noise I've left behind feels like it was my companion and defender, and now I am alone.

Anything might walk abroad in the tracklessness of my hush. And the fear of quiet is as old as Adam and as visceral as grief.

I think there's good reason for that kind of fear.

It might as well be said up front that when we step beyond the bright, frenzied circles of our distraction into the dark, waiting space of quiet, we end up meeting two people. The first is our own self, stripped, our need and fear in a raw welter upon our bare skin. Sometimes in quiet, the chill nakedness of our discontent and shame, our fear and desire, becomes plain to us in a way that leaves us almost breathless with dismay. There's a real sense in which the choice to be silent ushers us into the presence of all the things noise obscures for us most of the time: the inescapable nature of our frailty, the dreams we have lost, the hovering possibility of grief, our pervasive failure. To be quiet can feel like stepping into the presence of death.

Except for the fact that love has mapped the wilderness and waits at its heart; for the second person we meet in our quiet is God.

We are called to be a listening people.

How can we be otherwise?

In the beginning, before the tumult and song of history, before the spattered centuries of grieved desire and pain, before all the cries for love and justice unsettled the air and the world tumbled and twisted in a cacophony of anguished, ecstatic words, there was one radiant Word so beautiful it shattered the ancient and unformed darkness. This Word of God named and narrated us alive, spoke our battered, beautiful cosmos into being, and when it began it was wholly good.

In the beginning, we listened, and our listening was life itself.

When we now tell the story, in Genesis, of God calling out to Adam in the garden of Eden, it's usually tangled up with the tale of Adam's shame after he ate the apple. But I'm intrigued by the glimpse that daily calling gives us of what life looked like before the fall. Adam and Eve, unlimited by fear, unencumbered by pain, were offered the total freedom of an unblemished creation. Their world was luminous and safe, a feast crafted by divine love, and their vocation was to explore it as their kingdom and fill it as their home.

And every day God called them.

God came every day to talk with his people and called them by name, and this was before the fall. Can you imagine what it must have been like to be Eve, hands crusted in good dirt, face bathed in light, hearing the voice of the Almighty echo down the valley in desire of her company? What would they have talked about? Was every conversation the ground of new discovery for Adam and Eve, the invitation into a greater exploration of their image-bearing personhood? Did God tell them about music and help them start making it? Did he name the unformed secret ideas, the nascent hopes pushing up through the soil in their hearts (back when all secrets were good)? That daily conversation must have been the place in which they began to discover the innate capability of their own being and the comprehensive goodness in which it was cradled.

God's voice was the native soil of his people. And quiet was their homeland because in listening they entered afresh into the world-making words of God.

But that wondering, fertile hush was replaced with a voice that not only displaced the quiet but unraveled their capacity to listen. Sometimes it feels mad, unbearably mad, that the fall was instigated by a confusing conversation, but it was. Words

34

make worlds, and the words spoken by the snake to Eve shifted the landscape of her inner world so radically that she acted in direct opposition to the living Word who made her.

What did she gain? The more I read back through the story, the more I am convinced that all the serpent could promise was a knowledge of evil. He told them it was the knowledge of *good* and evil, but Adam and Eve, image-bearers of God, created from the overflow of God's generous love, walking amidst divine imagination enfleshed in the earth—they already *knew* all goodness. All they could gain was the knowledge of evil, the wary, grasping knowledge of all that opposes the goodness of God, all that elevates a faulty self, all that suspects the motives of any other. They yielded their great, blessed listening to the ranting, frantic voice of a world where all things suspect and compete with each other. They yielded the endless possibilities of conversation with God to the restless, competitive rage of a world in which every self wars against every other.

What does it feel like to bear the knowledge of evil? I sometimes wonder if it just means an unendingly disquiet mind.

Ever since that day, the human race has spent much of its history using noise to obscure the discord of that choice. To the racket of our fallenness we have added the rasping of our distraction so that we may forget how frail and terrified we have become. But in an age of media technology, we have raised this awful skill to a way of life. I am appalled sometimes to realize how much my own use of media technology is an unexamined effort to escape whatever makes me afraid. As a woman with OCD, I always have much to fear; I see what I fear has enacted in the intrusive thoughts that fill my mind each day. But worse than that, in a way, is the way I use my screens to distract myself from my insecurity, my sense of inadequacy, my loneliness and hunger. How many times in the last years of pandemic and sickness, of profound loneliness and loss, have I sat down for my first quiet moment and found myself so raw in the presence of quiet that I took up my phone as if it were a shield? Something to keep me from looking full-on at the emptiness I feel?

Humanity has never run short of ways to distract itself, but in the media age, distraction has become a way of life. I think the past years have seen an intensification of this engagement that threatens to destroy our capacity to relate to other people without suspicion, that sets us in a constant state of competition, that siphons away our sense of peace and bankrupts our capacity to accept anything at all as gift, or grace, or wonder.

I wonder if it's because our fear has become too great to face.

Life online these days reminds me of a party in F. Scott Fitzgerald's *The Great Gatsby*, all the "bright young things" wild and high on pleasure, on life in the now, their days a frenzied search for anything to distract them from the huge emptiness yawning beneath them. *Gatsby* was written by a man who was part of "the lost generation," those who returned home from the First World War to find all the landmarks of their hope and belief demolished by the horror they had witnessed in the trenches. They could not be quiet, they could not be still because of all they feared facing, because they were afraid the horror was ultimate, the loss of all things final.

It wasn't. It wasn't. Not for them and not for us.

Before and after and bearing all the horror is a beauty that will redeem and heal it. At the heart of our devastated silence is still that great Word speaking us back into life. He has never ceased to hover over the dark and unformed waters of our beings, speaking our names, his calling always an invitation to redemption.

But we have to listen.

We are invited to listen; quiet is never something that begins with us. It is always a response to the loving words of our Creator. That great Word spoke to us again when he took flesh, entered the cacophony of a fallen world, and, with his own final words—"It is finished"—began the story of love again. We enter quiet not just to hush our own voices but to hear his. And in the hearing, be saved.

When I first began writing this book, I thought of quiet as a rather demanding activity. I knew myself addicted to screens; I knew I was walking in patterns of fear and frenzy. I knew quiet was something I yearned for and something I was asked to do. I read many books by contemplatives; I planned out the hours I would spend in prayer (once my babies slept a little better). I made strict rules for myself regarding phones and screens. And none of this was bad—but none of it, so it would seem, was necessary to the growth of quiet in my life.

My past three years have been some of the least quiet in my life. Four young children, of course, do little to promote the discipline of silence, but the real obstacle to my quiet was my own spiritual exhaustion. As a family, we've lived through three years of major transitions and moves, of three births and three family deaths, of appendicitis and long Covid and severe asthma. And nowhere in the drama of those days did I ever manage to pray for more than ten minutes.

One morning last year, I sat at my desk for five silent, desperate minutes. We had reached the week before Easter, a period in which so often before I have known a deep spiritual joy in living out the drama of Christ's passion with our church. But that

Holy Week found us in self-isolation with Covid. My husband was scarily ill; I watched and nursed him even while our three young children coughed and clattered noisily about the house. The loneliness of that week prompted in me not an impulse to contemplation but a restless, distracted despair. I was afraid of the anger I would find in my quiet. Anger at God, at my inadequate self. I was also afraid that all quiet would reveal was my abandonment by a God I could not please.

On Good Friday, I sat at my desk and told God I had nothing to offer. I was not sure it was possible to live in quiet if it meant me doing yet one more hard, lonely thing. The whole history of my search for quiet seemed an unbearable burden. *Here's some quiet*, I breathed. *But don't ask me to pray. Don't ask me to repent. I only have five minutes, and I need something nourishing.* It was a kind of exhausted defiance. I pushed my prayer book aside and opened a book of poetry instead. There, to my immense startlement, I found a poem by Denise Levertov describing the way that God cradled her frailty. Her faith, her selfhood, she says, should break. Yet "minute by minute"[1] God kept her from falling.

And I sat, astonished into the listening I had avoided all week.

At the heart of my brief, inadequate, angry quiet I found the voice of my Maker telling me that I was already held before I cried out, that the fragile threads of self and psyche would not snap in his careful hands. I forgot to be afraid. At the heart of my quiet, beyond my many fears and the countless ways I distracted myself from them, was the love of God speaking me safe once more. The minute I listened, I discovered him there, all grace, again.

Have you ever noticed that when angels crash into a person's world in Scripture they almost always begin with the words "Do not be afraid"? I suppose that command could mean simply that angels are terrifying in aspect and appearance, but I'm inclined to think most messages from God begin with these words because we humans are so comprehensively afraid. What the angels are inviting us to with that phrase (because, of course, their words are in some sense a proclamation to us all) is to step into a story where fear is no longer necessary because God is telling the world right again. The living Word is still speaking as he did at creation. He speaks the incarnate Word of Christ. He fills us with the undying voice of his own Holy Spirit. And he speaks to us what the angels have always spoken. At the heart of our quiet, we will find the voice that says, "Do not fear, for I have redeemed you; I have called you by name; you are Mine!"[2]

What might it mean to be at home, even now, in the voice of God?

In my study, I have a print of a painting by a local artist hanging over my fireplace. It's an intricate impressionist sketch in black and white, splashed with pale blue, of a woman with her face hidden in her hands. There's a sadness to it; it's not hard to think she's grieving, as several visitors have pointed out. Yet she's cradled in a great burst of gold. She can't see it, but she's wholly encircled by a circle of radiance. When she lifts her face, I often think, whenever she gathers the courage, she'll finally realize that the great silence attending her sorrow is leading her to the quiet presence of her Lover, the one waiting to speak her back to joy.

At the end of darkness, at the heart of quiet, there is love.

I've spent a year now looking out the vicarage window. The silence still seems a little void when I begin, but I am learning to dwell in the simple grace of listening. I've gotten in the habit of letting a little music play. These days I'm loving the choral work in *The Lost Birds* by Christopher Tin. I let the quiet settle. Sink myself into the comfort and hush of the music. Sometimes I simply fall asleep, but even that, I've come to realize, is one of the ways God sets me back into the safety and quiet for which I yearn. I listen. And I breathe. I find his breath at the base of my own, calling me to life.

And those long, dark nights when I was a child? Yes, at first I was afraid. But when the adrenaline finished its gallop and my breath began to slow, I found my sight widened and changed. The night moved near, not in threat but in softness, a world of gentle sounds, a multitude of blazing stars that astonished my sight. I felt myself merge with the great quiet, felt it enter skin and breath. Perhaps that was when I first tasted the holy call to quiet, because while I couldn't yet name it, what I felt was a great kindness brooding at the back of that vast, gorgeous darkness with myriad stars and the piping of night birds and the rustle of grass.

In that quiet, I was no longer afraid.

I was home.

Pray

O Whisperer, who spoke us first alive and told our story bright and sweet, help us to hear your voice again. From all the rancor and rage of the world, deliver us, defend us, so that we may hear the kindness of your own sweet voice anew. Give us courage to enter the wilderness of hush and trust your love to defend us against the sorrow and need that stalk our way. When the darkness looms large, help us to look up and find the constellations of your love. Be gentle with us as we learn again to listen, as we enter once more the world-making joy of your voice. Through the love of our Lord, Jesus Christ, Amen.

Ponder

- Set aside ten minutes for a space of real quiet. Do not allow yourself any other distraction or aid. What rises in the silence? What troubles or grieves you?
- Set aside a separate space of quiet for a different practice: listen for God's voice. It may not come in the way you think; it may come to mind as a quote or Scripture, it may come as warmth or relief, it may come, for all you know, as audibly as your own, but let yourself enter a place of hopeful listening once more.

3

Trust amidst Apocalypse

Peace

We called it our hobbit season because we spent most of our spare moments in the garden. And if we weren't grubbing about with roses and slugs, we were probably baking; I learned to knead bread by hand with my second new baby (Samuel, named in part for Sam Gamgee) tucked in a sling, the gentle rhythm rocking him to sleep. We baked daily fresh bread and scones to go with the new strawberries, and brownies to celebrate the blossoming of the first rose we'd raised by our own good, earthy work.

Springtime that year was early and lush, and the hills near our home were blanketed in golden buttercups and celandine, fragile pink primroses, and lacy branches of hawthorn. We lived in the Sussex downs, a gull's cry to the seashore and a five-minute walk to the undulating hills with their mazed trails and brambly hedges. The sun shone at least a little most days, and we spent them outdoors with our two small children; in the garden, on a quilt, with picnic baskets and picture books. When evening set in and the long day finally drew down to shadow, Thomas and I would sit in the garden with glasses of wine, watching the moonrise and the dart of the night birds across the horizon.

It was a season almost ideal in its pastoral cadence, in the fellowship we knew as a young family and the flourishing we saw in our small children—except for the fact that it happened amidst a worldwide pandemic. The peaceful hours of each day were punctuated by our obsessive checking of our phones as Covid swept the world and everything went into lockdown. I remember vividly the days leading up to the pandemic, because I was barely past Samuel's birth. I was up countless times at night to feed him, checking my phone as the headlines began to moan and scream with the rising tide of woe: 2:00 a.m., pandemic declared; 4:00 a.m., borders closing; 6:00 a.m., a world we barely knew how to navigate.

My husband's work life changed suddenly and oddly intensified as his church shifted entirely to online provision, and he had to learn a host of new technologies in order to make it all possible. We watched borders close and knew the grief of watching the family who'd felt a brief plane ride away from meeting the new baby and helping us in that transitional season become suddenly unreachable. Friends canceled long-planned holidays to see us. Our local town went silent, shops and restaurants closed, and only the grocery stores were open for brief, stressful shopping. I bore the fragility of sleepless young motherhood and struggled not to lose myself in the rising tide of loneliness and woe.

I think that's why we bought those three first roses. Thomas and I both recognized our need to do something creative in the yawning, lonely hours that opened wide around us with a rest-less toddler and a curious baby. We found those plants, a little bedraggled, on a rack stuffed with dying flowers as we stood in a long line waiting for masked, distanced entrance into a grocery store. Neither of us were sure the plants would make it, but we carted them home and dragged them out to the little square of garden we called our own in that season.

Thing is, that garden was a holy mess. When first we'd come to rent the house in the summer of the year before, the grass had grown so scratchy and high our daughter wouldn't even venture out the door. We'd finally managed to mow it all down, but the beds were still tangled with weeds, and the stone walls had mostly toppled in the spring rains that came just after our son's birth. We didn't have an overly attentive landlord, so when we carted those roses home, we realized abruptly that we had a lot of work to do.

But what else, really, was there to do? In the absence of any social gathering, we took ourselves to the garden. Thomas re-built the stone beds brick by brick. We piled in new soil and raked it into the old, clumpy dirt, and after much watering, we finally took those roses and patted them into the ground as gently as we might put our new baby in his bed.

But those roses seemed to demand all sorts of new improve-ments; we pulled countless hundreds of weeds by hand from the gaps in the beautiful, burnished old stone paths. We cleared the fence lines and trimmed the bushes. We managed to find a few old chairs and a table, and we set them up on the little raised platform at the back of the garden so we could watch our roses and guard the lupines against the slugs.

The headlines kept screaming, Covid spread, our loneliness grew. But so did our roses. So did our pride in the order we were making in our one little corner of the world. However mighty the news of disaster, we found ourselves capable of creating gracious hours, of cultivating roses and lupines, rosemary and strawberries, of drawing our children into the rich normalcy of the springtime world. We found ourselves capable of a careful, chosen joy.

And I found myself filled with a mighty tension.

The headlines I read each hour, on my phone, left me feeling that it was my duty to focus on disaster. I wanted so much to give my full presence to that golden season, but I felt such attention was something I could only access or allow myself on the other side of trouble. Along with the rest of the waking world, I spent a good portion of each day scrolling countless websites and social media feeds for news. I read the stories of death. I saw the statistics of disease. There was a sense of solidarity in sharing the fear and woe. But there was also a real danger of unraveling.

Trying to bear the outrage, the loneliness, the fear of countless strangers left me sleepless and strung out in the deep nights, clutching my baby, unable to feast on the swiftly changing beauty of his new little face because a phone screen glimmered and boiled just beyond it. I fixed my eyes upon anguish and angst, and soon found that quiet was something I could no longer reach.

———————

There will never *not* be a crisis.

One apocalypse or another is always underway in the wider world and in our own lives. Suffering, fear, straight- up trouble are the conditions in which both our faith and the quiet in which we root it will be sought. It is easy to think of both peace and quiet as things to be found on the other side of turmoil, gifts that depend upon the absence of unrest and fear.

But "Peace I leave with you, My peace I give to you," Jesus says, and it is a peace "not as the world gives."[1]

What is the peace of the world? Perhaps we would call it security or safety; the sense that physical walls and human strength, burgeoning bank accounts and spending capacity, or healthy bodies and modern medicine make us powerful enough to enact and ensure peace for ourselves. When those things fail, when we ourselves crumble in illness or crisis, when a pandemic unravels society, the peace of the world is no longer something we may acquire because it was always something to be bought. And sooner or later, we will all find ourselves impoverished by suffering.

The peace given by Jesus is entirely a gift.

But what does it mean to get our hands round that peace, the kind of trust that is a homecoming and a rest, a quiet that suffuses the whole of self and soul?

In his remarkable work *The Beauty of the Infinite*, theologian David Bentley Hart describes the story of Christianity as "a word of peace whose ultimate promise is also peace."[2] This is a story that directly challenges the violence and cruelty of so much of fallen human history. But, he wrote urgently, Christianity's claim is even greater; we believe that this word of peace enters into the violence of history not as an idea but as a Person. "The peace of God—the shalom of creation . . . has a real shape and presence, a concrete story, one which has entered into human history as a contrary history, the true story God always tells."[3]

Shalom, as a larger description of societal peace and spiritual renewal, is a concept that radiates throughout Scripture. With a root meaning of "completeness, soundness, welfare, peace,"[4] it has the connotations I think we often hear in the much-clichéd phrase "world peace," this idea of the cosmos and all the peoples within it returned to an original harmony. These days I think we often assume shalom just means everyone giving each other kindly space to live their own lives, but the Christian idea of shalom is much greater. The pervasive, cosmic peace we crave is a real force flowing from the Trinity, the fellowship of divine affection and generosity from whose overflow the whole of our existence was made. It settles wars, heals what is broken, redeems what is lost. And just as Hart said, the concrete embodiment of that peace has entered our history in the person of Jesus.

When Jesus gives us *his* peace, it means he gives us himself.

That doesn't exempt us from struggle here in the broken place; it promises us an alternate story singing in the midst of our darkness, a story that shows us a different way to live in the face of pain, that leads us to quiet in the midst of the storm and shows us the hard and holy road of hope. Jesus made the promise of peace to his disciples on the very eve of his death, in John 14. He opens that passage by telling them not to let their hearts "be troubled" because, I think, he knew how great and natural the urge to be profoundly, even wildly troubled would be. Those disciples were about to watch Jesus suffer a brutal execution. Everything they knew and believed about who Jesus was, his power to save, his identity as God's chosen one, would be challenged in the hours that followed.

But Jesus, the Prince of Peace, would, for the sake of their peace and the sake of ours, bear all the brutal, wounding troubledness of human history so he could bring about the shalom of the entire world. His peace, not as the world gives but as he gives, himself. The one we find waiting in the quiet before and after every disaster, the Peace who began our stories and will see them to a gracious end.

———————————

In the Anglican churches where I now worship, Maundy Thursday is one of the great services in the Triduum, the last three days of Holy Week that lead up to the festival celebrations of Easter morning. I didn't grow up in this tradition, but I have come to deeply love the holy drama. The Triduum is a way of entering the story of Jesus's passion, sharing it with him but also remembering that this is the story of our own lives. We walk his grief and ours and live the passionate suffering of a fallen world, but because we walk it in his presence, we walk it with him to life.

The Triduum begins with an evening service for Maundy Thursday, a commemoration of the Last Supper, when Jesus washed the feet of his disciples. The Eucharist is celebrated and the priest reenacts the great humility of Christ by washing the feet of some congregants. There's a different lot every year; always a giggling bunch of children, baring their feet with enviable abandon. Always a few adults, shyer, stocking feet tucked under their chairs until the last moment. I always feel the service opens in a sort of camaraderie; the candles are lit, everyone's there to live the story, and the priest has to wash a bunch of grubby feet.

But the end of that service always bears an element of dread. For just like Jesus and his disciples on the night before his death, we leave the cozy enclosure of the upper room. We, as they did, venture out into the perilous night. For at the end of the service, the priest bears the eucharistic bread away from the table and the congregation follows, usually to a side chapel or alcove.

As we go, all the candles are snuffed and the altars stripped. Where usually we see rich, old cloths covering the tables and candles casting a gentle light, now there is nothing, only bare wood and angular stone and shadow. The stripping is meant to signal that we are entering the story of the crucifixion, when all we can rely upon in the outward world is brutally taken away.

I feel that stripping viscerally every year. The first time I witnessed it, watched the church grow abruptly dark with the rustling of cloths and cassocks like an evil storm wind sweeping everything comforting and good away, I was a student in a time of crisis, with doubts pounding my mind and loneliness wrecking my heart. The second time was mere days after the loss of my first little baby to miscarriage; I'd seen his form, precious and unreachably lifeless on the ultrasound. I'd lost him. He had been stripped from my body. I already knew the stripping of death when I came to the service that year, and there is a sense in which it echoes in me each Triduum that I celebrate.

But light endures even in that great darkness because Christ sojourns with us. Where Christ is, symbolized by the eucharistic bread, the priest and congregation light as many candles as we can and gather in a circle of watchful prayer. Every year, vigil is kept until late, late on that Maundy Thursday as people kneel and pray deep into the night. At one level of symbolism, this vigil is a way we offer Jesus the company his disciples refused him by their sleep. "Watch with me," pleads the agonized Jesus of the Gospels, sweating blood in his dread of all that would be stripped from him in the coming hours.

But every year, I cannot escape the feeling that I am also being sheltered. The whole church, the whole world is shrouded in black, but here we are in the garden with Jesus, and the story of his suffering is the story of our refuge. Even as we offer him our prayer, he covers us in a peace the world has never been able to give. I have spent some of the quietest, deepest moments of prayer in my life in the circled candlelight of the Maundy Thursday vigil. Even in his agony, Jesus brings me peace, is agonized precisely for my peace, so that the story of my agony is not final.

In the days after I lost my baby, I walked and walked and walked the river trails round Oxford. My shoes were muddy from early spring rain. Fragile blossoms starred the wet branches, a few crocuses nosed up through the moldy fallen leaves of the year before. I found the sight almost painful. My own babe's body had been fragile and gorgeous like those flowers. But as I walked, I played one song in my earphones again and again, Audrey Assad's "Even Unto Death." She composed it in honor of the Egyptian Christians beheaded by ISIL on video in 2015. The song is a prayer to Jesus, "lover of my soul, even unto death," the final apocalypse, and it echoed in my ears as I walked, grieving the death of my baby.

But the words also sang in my heart as I knelt that year at the Maundy Thursday vigil, as I sheltered in the undying light of Jesus's peace throughout the drama of the Triduum. There, the tumult of my sorrow fell away, and a vast quiet took me in its arms. The death of my baby was no less grievous, but he and I both were caught up in the arms of a love that could not be touched or changed by any apocalypse, even death itself. And the quiet that came was the hushed breath of trust, the kind a child breathes when the fear—of darkness or solitude or monsters—has left them and they relax, limp and beloved, into the arms of the parent who has saved them.

The peace of Jesus, unlike any other in the world.

———

I did, eventually, find that peace in the quiet of our hobbit season.

As spring waxed late that pandemic year in Sussex, I woke one morning in a kind of exhausted defeat. I looked at my new baby, following the lines of his face with my finger, for ah, new babies change so quickly. Already his cheekbones showed a little firmer beneath his soft skin; already the starry grey mists of his eyes were hardening into deep, oceanic blue.

And I put my phone away.

I turned my face toward the quiet I needed in order to attend to the grace that was before and all around me.

I made some baby steps to help myself; the first was simply to wake to something besides a screen, to gulls crying and birds singing, a line of Scripture, a fragrant cup of coffee sipped with the babes by the window before any hint of the online world. From that small choice came the possibility of simply stretching out the hours before I looked at my phone. I tried a similar space of screen-free time before bed, letting my mind wind down to a kind of watchful, deep-breathed hush. It was hard at times. I failed often, and yet, in the days following those tiny choices, I recognized a gradual quieting of my mind.

My consciousness subtly shifted as I rooted myself in the hush of that season.

The hobbit life we were living took on a significance I had somehow missed. The downs in their springtime luxuriance, the hedges peppered with valerian, the fields starred with buttercups—their beauty wasn't a neutral distraction, peripheral to the suffering at large in the world. They were a kind of answer and defiance, an order and loveliness that endured, that had grown up amidst and after disaster and would again. Our garden was our participation in the larger pageantry of their grace, a choice to plant, to tend, to work for the satedness of both soul and stomach by the creation of growth in the face of catastrophe. The picnics with our small ones, the bowls of strawberries and endless picture books, the cultivation of innocence in the very face of its loss in the wider world; these were our way of rooting ourselves in that ancient, holy peace that endures beyond all disasters and will heal the grief they bring.

Our hobbit life was not a denial of disorder and pain or a refusal to engage those things where we could. Rather it was a refusal to allow those forces to define our story or that of the world. In those months, I recognized in a new and visceral way the power of that life to offer me a practical, embodied way to live in opposition to panic. I could plant peace. I could cultivate quiet. I could resist the unraveling of the world with beauty. I could root myself in a goodness much larger than the furor and tumult I saw each day in the online world.

What could I do in that season to help that tumult? Nothing.

Except to plant my garden and love my children.

Except to bake my bread and write another letter to a lonely friend.

Except to watch another long, sinuous day unfold itself in golden splendor over the downs and climb to the top of the hill to witness its hope.

Except . . . to pray. Like the saints through the ages in times of plague and famine and war, when there was nothing to be done except trust that God would arrive, merciful, amidst the storm. And what is trust except a kind of quiet attention?

I think that's the season in which, amidst many other seeds, this book planted itself as a living desire in my mind, because I began to question what it means to be at peace in the midst of disaster, to be rooted in a quiet larger than the roaring tumult of the world. Quiet, then, began to seem rather necessary to a robust life of faith: not just its fruit, not just a benefit to be found in seasons of rest, but its very foundation.

Why quiet amidst apocalypse?

Because my faith is driven by the belief that I have found my rest in a goodness that will outlast the apocalypse, this one and every other.

Because mercy is unceasing and so must my gratitude be.

Because beauty in her countless garments does not cease to defy the darkness and heal the broken world.

Because God does not change and his kindness does not end, though the mountains shift and whole worlds crumble, and to actually believe this means to live a different kind of life from one tossed and overturned by news of every new disaster.

Because quiet is, truly, the proclamation of my citizenship—even here in the storm winds, even now in the grief—in a kingdom whose peace cannot be threatened, whose joy will not fail to overturn all the weeping of the world.

Pray

O God, who does not fail though all the world be tumbling, help us to hold you fast. From the whirlwind of our fear, draw us into the shelter of your peace. Help us to root our hearts in a world and hope much larger than the tempests of the present time, to anchor our minds in the love that began us and will once more see us whole. Help us to find the disciplines of hope so that joy is a thing we can taste like an apple and peace can be a candle we may light in the night. Let quiet lead us daily into trust, through the grace of our Lord, Jesus Christ, Amen.

Ponder

- What are the "apocalypses" in your own life? What storms threaten you deeply, what disasters have unmoored you from a sense of God's care?
- What would it mean for you to find a sense of refuge where your hope might be restored? On a spiritual level? And even on a physical one?
- What beauty have you encountered that summons you to trust?

4

Lover's Quest

Pilgrimage

The world was a canvas painted all in a palette of grey as I set out.

I drove; the road was a dark ribbon beneath me, the dying fields out the window already sere and wintered. It looked like some malicious spirit had siphoned all the color from the world so that the stripped, brown trees scratched a monotone sky. My friend slept deeply in the seat next to me, and I was glad. Despondence wants no company. There were few things I was certain of in my life, but I was a smooth, sure driver, and I sped westward, my back to the rising sun, the hum of the car making a cocoon of undisturbed quiet all around me.

I, too, was barren in the silence, unable to hide from myself anymore. I had come to the end of a journey that had been started in part to outrun an almost ravenous hunger for . . . what, I couldn't always name. A more shaped life whose meaning and destination were evident to me, certainly. I felt I'd been waiting for years for something to happen, some love to root me or some great work to drive me. But the hunger I felt was for something even larger, and I'd chased it up six thousand miles of highway for over a month.

Some years earlier, in my hungering twenties, when the first hint of autumn chilled the mountains, I took my tiny blue hatchback and bolted all the way from the hills of Colorado to the eastern coasts of Canada. If anyone asked, I said I was traveling to literary sites in North America as research for a book. Which I was. But I went on that road trip in much the same spirit a grieved child might run away from home.

I was very quiet as I drove. The open land of the plains stretched wide around me. Each day I rose before the sun and drove into the dawn. Fawns gamboled in the cornfields. Leaves began to shiver and burn as the miles galloped by under my tires. For many days I barely spoke to anyone, except my family occasionally on the phone, or friends when I stayed the night with them, or the desk staff at roadside motels.

There were no smartphones in those ancient days, and I listened to a great deal of aching violin music. I had just watched a strange film with my brother called *The Village*, M. Night Shyamalan's weird mix of period drama and contemplative novel and horror film, a story exploring what humans will do to hedge themselves away from suffering. I listened to the soundtrack from that film as I drove the long cornfields of Iowa and felt my soul rise to the cry of the violins as I pondered the questions asked by the film. Can we escape from pain, or is it within us? Is suffering ultimate, or is love? Are we left to kick and cry like a baby abandoned in the darkness, or is there some compassion actually cradling us after all?

I wasn't yet sure. Chicago, Ohio, New York—I drove and drove, and the travel wasn't a chase but a suspension, a place where I let my need for a world and a self far better than I had yet known find its voice. I was so, so hungry for a thousand things and for God and for life itself, as if it were a food I couldn't find because I could not give it a name.

———————

Years later, I sat in my priest's tiny study. The light was low as always, the kind that filters in through thick forest. Bookshelves loomed tall like old trees, the pages of a thousand books filling my mind with a kind of rustling like leaves. A scent not incongruent with that idea, something woodsy and fragrant, calmed me as I waited in the low, leather chair.

I had much to untangle in those days, and the priest and counselor whose office this was became a formal companion to me in the difficult work of that season. I found myself, during our regular talks, not interrogated but made capable of tracing and articulating burdens and griefs I did not know I had carried, had not been able to express. Joys, too, sometimes.

One day as we talked, he asked me about the road trips I had taken throughout my twenties. Those years of intense OCD saw me severely limited by anxiety in so many ways, incapable of leaving home or forging normal patterns of adult life, and yet strangely able to embark upon weeks of independent, solitary travel. I'd driven thousands of miles cross-country in the blue hatchback I'd scraped and saved to buy. I didn't really know how to articulate those journeys at first. They were an exception. A kind of miracle. I stuttered in trying to describe them. I was so shamed and hungry, in those years, for all I could not manage, for all the things I could not do, for the life I feared would never begin. To slip into the predawn darkness and race down the Colorado highways, to be utterly silent, cocooned in quiet, to watch the light and the sere landscapes shift and grow outside my window allowed me a blessed kind of suspension in which I could simply yearn.

"But then, I guess I've always wanted more than the ordinary could give me."

My words slipped out in the quiet of the office and startled me.

The moment was one of epiphany.

Mental illness or not, I've always borne a hunger for something that seemed as distant as starlight and as wide as the night sky itself. I want the world and I want what is behind it, the potent beauty it simultaneously reveals and veils. I think we all do, and the spacious quiet of my road trips allowed me a startling grasp of this essential aspect of my nature. I was suspended from the need to act as if the foibles and fetters of workaday life were enough. They weren't. There were no pretenses or pressures in those trips. In the absolute silence of my car, I was allowed to know not only the smaller sorrows of my circumstances but the larger ache that showed me to myself as the pilgrim I was.

I turned, startled, to my priest.

"Your body language has completely changed," my friend said, smiling, as I stumbled into this realization. "Your breathing has eased. There's a light in your face."

Don't we all want more than the world can give us?

And where shall we go to remember that this hunger is holy?

I've thought often of that moment as I've wrestled with the nature of quiet and what it asks us to understand about ourselves. At first, I found myself frustrated by the paradoxical nature of the understanding that came to me in travel. If there is one thing I have come to deeply believe in the past ten years of spiritual excavation, it is that escaping the ordinary is no escape. If I cannot find "earth crammed with heaven"[1] in the forced bulb growing in winter on my windowsill, I will not find it in whole fields of blossoms in abandoned, springtime wandering. I truly believe it's amidst our ordinary stuff that the divine affection cradling our lives is both revealed and enfleshed: in our fierce little acts of kindness, in our humble creations, in moments of intricate and miniature beauty or words offered like water in the tiny deserts of our individual loneliness.

And yet.

There is a potent grace in spaces of suspension when the pilgrim nature of our lives finds expression in a period of seeking. We're all born hungry, so hungry. We don't always remember this, but the broken world around us was never the one for which we were originally made. At the back of our happiest moments here is the haunting strain of a music that draws us onward, beyond any good we have ever known.

Our hunger is integral to our discipleship.

My road trips were a life-changing space because they gave me a certain freedom in prayer. The vast quiet of those hours allowed me an honesty in expressing my deep need I had not allowed myself amidst the tumble of my homebound days. I was always traveling in company with Christ; he was the Companion and he was the Way, as I was to discover. The great quiet of the road allowed me to address him with unvarnished desire. I think that's why my body language changed in describing those days; even in memory, I entered a different way of being when I inhabited the widened mental borders of that traveling space. The pilgrim nature, not just of my mentally ill life but of my personhood, my human hunger for something more than the broken world, was given expression in those spaces of movement and quest.

But my road trips are not the only place I've known that holy suspension, that freedom to search. They taught me to value my hunger, but they also revealed the great spaciousness of quiet itself as the condition for such quests. In that season, I needed the physical differentiation of the open road in order to discover the quiet available to me. But quiet was always there. It remains, ever a pilgrim space at the very heart of my ordinary, one that continues to bear an epiphanic quality similar to the lightening and insight I found on my journeys. Quiet, ah, it is so often the place of our pilgrimage, the place we come to discover our hunger and honor it by a journey not measured in miles but by the growing fixity of our inward attention as we set off in quest of the Love our hearts so ravenously desire.

———

Have you ever interrogated your yearning? I know you have it; we all bear unmet desire. Not just for love or safety, success or approval, though all those earthy, human things gesture to the larger things we're missing. We desire something we can't quite name, a deeper satisfaction than we have ever found in any one thing or person in this world.

Have you ever allowed yourself to sit in the presence of that secret, inconsolable longing? Have you endured the pain of it until a light began to rise amidst the darkness? Have you stood like a watchman on the walls of your heart through the witching hour of dusk when the horizons of productivity and familiarity give way to some vast realm just beyond your understanding, a realm that is both your terror and your deep desire?

No?

Then come into the quiet, for here you will learn the holy work of hunger and the way it prods us onto the heaven-bound road.

It is a truth universal but rarely acknowledged that human beings are born into a state of pilgrimage. We are, by nature, seekers. This broken world isn't the one we were born for, and we're looking for the native ground of our inmost hope all the days of our busy, ambitious lives. That's not usually the first way we describe ourselves or measure the outlines of a good life, but it's the reality thrumming beneath every pattern of human existence on this earth.

This truth, though, is obscured by our modern plethora of outward distraction, our capacity to drown silence in noise, to fill every solitary moment with entertainment. We have been born into a world so drained of quiet that we may almost endlessly ignore or obscure our longing in the amusements and things and accomplishments that crowd our days. We have limitless choices, and as author Charles Taylor points out in his sweeping exploration of what it means to live in "a secular age," that makes any decision profoundly fraught.[2] Our smartphones can answer all our questions. We can order any good we lack at the click of a button. We need never be alone, for Siri is with us and she never sleeps.

And why would we seek a quiet in which all we might find at first is the awful shape of an ache we do not know how to heal? Why seek solitude and silence if those things might unravel our capacity to reach, run, and perform all the activities keeping us from the despair of naming a desire we've come to think can never be answered?

But our pilgrim state, however painful it often feels, is actually a life-giving condition, one meant to reveal to us the greater good for which we were so lovingly created. In quiet we find not just our own nameless hunger but a presence reaching out to us from beyond the walls of this world. Quiet echoes with eternity; it thrums with the music of the world we've always secretly desired but have only just begun to imagine.

C. S. Lewis, in his sermon "The Weight of Glory," said our yearning is an "inconsolable secret," one that hurts us so deeply we are embarrassed to admit it and conceal it by relegating such hunger to the realm of teenage idealism or childlike awe.[3] But our hunger haunts us throughout our lives.

I wasn't ashamed of my hunger when I was a child. I thrilled to it. There were moments—I called them "knowings"—when I knew an almost unbearable joy in a moment of beauty. In the accidental cloister of a summer's day spent alone in the Texas fields, in a line of Celtic music heard when I was eight, in some of the stories I so hungrily read, I "knew" something about God, about his kindness and closeness to me, that I could not explain in ordinary words. As a teenager, this knowing combined with a passionate yearning for meaning that left me scratching out anguished poems to "homes I'd never seen" and "faces I'd loved without sight."

In my teens, I soon discovered that Lewis and I were not the only ones who bore this secret experience. I could trace it through countless pages in the literature I loved. While Lewis spoke of a "Joy" evoked by literature and beauty that was both his anguish and his treasure, Tolkien wrote of "joy beyond the walls of the world, poignant as grief," tasted in the fairy tales and myths that startle us with hope.[4] I found it in Lisel Mueller's aching poem about a young girl who weeps with desire and joy upon hearing a piece of great music and doesn't know why.[5] It's in Willa Cather's description of her fierce soprano heroine Thea Kronborg, who hears a portion of a Dvořák symphony and encounters an "ecstasy" that "she would live for . . . work for . . . die for."[6] I even found it when I came to study theology and stumbled upon Charles Taylor's description of a "moment of fullness" when we taste a kind of life that "is fuller, richer, deeper, more worthwhile, more admirable, more what it should be."[7]

What I learned in these discoveries is that to hunger profoundly, to yearn for something that seems almost cosmic in the heft of its absence within our hearts is a holy thing. It is an integral part of seeking what is ultimate and meaningful, what hovers at the edge of human existence, beckoning us to a completion we have only begun to imagine.

At our truest, we are all of us pilgrims at all times of our lives. But it takes a little quiet to remember this.

In the spacious, suspended place of quiet, we are recalled to our true selves, summoned to examine and honor this eternal impulse within us. To watch and wait; this is integral to the shape and practice of quiet and to the health of our souls. In some sense it is fundamental to our lives as Christians. We are always waiting and seeking the return of our King. We chase his real presence even as we wait to receive it, and the quiet, the stillness in which we journey, is fundamental to the hunger that will define our lives.

But what do we do with our hunger?

One year when I was a teenager, my parents gave me a *Strong's Concordance* for Christmas. It was a nerdy but magnificent gift, one I've used countless times over the years. I am fascinated by the different connotations and subtle meanings many Hebrew and Greek words in Scripture bear, a nuance often lost in their translation to English. That old concordance came to my aid again recently as I tried to understand what it is we're supposed to do with all our pilgrim angst when we enter a space of quiet. Those beautiful songs of David and others in Psalms are peppered with commands to "wait on the Lord," to watch, to rest, to hope in his Word, all gesturing to this state of poised expectancy that is a kind of sublimated action. So one day I looked up the word *wait* and other words used to describe this waiting in some of my favorite (by which I mean most desperately prayed) psalms:

Psalm 25:21: "I wait for You."

Psalm 27:14: "Wait for the Lord; be strong and let your heart take courage."

Psalm 37:34: "Wait for the Lord and keep His way."

Psalm 40:1: "I waited patiently for the Lord; and He . . . heard my cry."

Psalm 52:9: "I will wait on Your name, for it is good."

I discovered that *wait*, as used in many of these psalms, means not to passively bide one's time but to "look for, hope, expect," to "look eagerly for," and, even more intriguingly, to "bind together" or "be collected" (the same word used in Genesis 1:9 to describe God's gathering together of the waters on the third day of creation).[8]

What is it that we gather when we come to the pilgrimage of quiet?

I've found this question a powerful one as I examine the worth in seeking quiet spaces. The "waiting" in each psalm is couched in the psalmist's need. We wait because we cannot save ourselves. Because the enemy is strong and cruel. Because we are not the source of our own blessing and there is so, so much that we desire. Because we yearn for the King in his beauty. And in that waiting, we gather up these hungry needs and recognize that the pitted and pocked world we know cannot be all we were made for. We cup our desires in our hands, turn them over, and name them. And then we hope for God's arrival. We expect his help to march up over the far horizon, ready to save us from whatever hunger or disaster broods at our backs. We expect him to fulfill the great, eternal ache at the center of our inmost selves.

———————

On that long-ago autumn trip, I picked up a friend in Boston because my parents had gotten worried about me and insisted I take on a travel companion. I loved her dearly but felt each day a little less capable of hope and, with it, conversation. We did our best to revel and explore, searching out old villages and cafés, walking the coasts, exploring the red sand cliffs. But by the morning of our departure, I felt rubbed raw, incapable of normal interaction.

A few days before, the news of the West Nickel Mines school shooting of eleven Old Order Amish girls had broken. Five were killed and six seriously wounded; some of the girls asked to be shot first in order to spare their little sisters and friends. A darkness had grown in me for days. There was something about the innocence and courage of those girls that tortured me, that made my sense of the world's darkness, my own hunger for healing and meaning, almost unbearable.

So when we began the drive home, my friend slept and I grieved. And the horizon behind me showed not a hint of light.

To keep myself awake, I put on an old Fernando Ortega album I'd listened to as travel music for years. The songs slipped by as the light slowly grew. I didn't really look anywhere else but up the dull, grey highway wending through half-lit fields. I prayed, but only in the sense that my ache was directed in some vague way toward God, until a line from one of the songs broke suddenly into my consciousness.

"O Jerusalem . . ."

I'd always found that song strange. Ortega seems to have written a lament about this holy city, soaked in blood, this "bride of the prophets" whose story yet seems to be always a tragedy. It's not the kind of song one can explain so much as experience, but as the mournful lyrics and yearning music thrummed in my little car, it seemed to give wonderful voice to the sorrow I felt, my profound frustration with a world always producing martyrs and victims and never living up to the promise of its beauty. But even as I listened, a subtle change came into my mind. I became aware of the song as the cry not just of one human musician or even his listeners but of God himself, whose city Jerusalem is. The blind, battered city was a symbol for the whole of God's shattered world. And the words of Christ in Luke filled my thoughts, the actual cry of the God who came to save this city on a hill:

> O Jerusalem, Jerusalem, the city that kills the prophets and stones those sent to her! How often I wanted to gather your children together, just as a hen gathers her brood under her wings, and you would not have it![9]

At that moment, in the startled breath provoked by what I found in the song, I finally looked up from the grey road and glanced in my rearview mirror. I was astonished by the sight. A crimson sky met my eyes. Not a cloud or two of ruby or a bit of rosy mist but a literal wall of flaming crimson stretched across the eastern horizon. The color rippled westward as the sun rose so that the crimson began to tinge the low clouds out the windows to my left and right. It was apocalyptic light, shattering light, unbearable, threatening, a benevolent beauty so great I could barely meet its gaze as it gradually enveloped the whole of the landscape around me. Fields shimmered, trees burned, birds glittered with its flame.

I was astonished.

The blood of that sky, the pulse of that light; it was as if the song had taken form in their terrible beauty. This was the world God had made, and now the whole of it pulsed with the keening of its Maker, a God who saw and bore the deaths of small girls and the weeping of their mothers and the dramatic angst of a minor, frustrated pilgrim like me. The light sang with his grief and the music pulsed with his own vast hunger, his own unbounded yearning for the people made in his image to turn from their wicked ways and know his love.

I don't remember how many times I listened to that song or how long that crimson light lasted; the road through that province was flat as could be, but in my memory I mounted from peak to peak in the brilliance of that color and song. They "gathered to a greatness," as Hopkins would say, all about me as I sped forward into a loveliness that broke my heart and an understanding that would shape my life.[10]

Before my own heart ever learned its hungry cry, the hunger of God himself cried out for me.

No grief escapes his eye, no tear slips from his hand. As God incarnate, he cried in anguish over his city; he reached out his arms on the cross in his hunger to hold the whole of his stubborn, shattered little world. Our pilgrim hunger is simply our response to the ever-present keening of God over his people, a summoning our desire does not instigate but answer. In the hunger I knew in those aching days of travel, in the anguished spaces of quiet, I discovered the prior and vast hunger of God for the healing of the world.

I traveled on. I drove and drove and drove, chasing the light figuratively once that sunrise faded, listening for that ancient, grieving love. I drove for at least another week, but the exultation of that morning did not depart from my heart. The fire in the sunrise leapt into the trees; I followed the sweep of autumn south down the Great Smoky Mountains, awed by the sight of whole mountains set aflame by the turning of the leaves. That fire, it was pure and clean, and every day as I drove and listened and prayed it burned away the bitterness of my hunger. The hunger itself remained, made clean by the love that kindled it. For God's hunger is first a holy force that draws our hearts homeward and finds its satisfaction in meeting every need we bear.

That hunger has followed me all of my days.

My traveling days are limited now; silence just doesn't stretch around me in quite the same way with four small ones in tow. But there are still those pockets of pilgrim quiet. Sometimes at night, when the wind blows in the darkness and quiet blooms in the shadows, I sit by my window alone and let my soul stretch itself out to the love that keeps me walking through a broken world, to the light that kindles my hope, to the voice that keens and sings me forward, step by step, into the new world where all my hunger will end.

Pray

O God, *whose love is the root of all our yearning, teach us to treasure our hunger. Draw us onto the pilgrim path, let foot and soul be restless to find you. Help us to enter the quiet we find each day as the place of our adventuring. Help us to search, help us to yearn, and lead us not, we pray, into any dark valley of despair. Day by day, let our going in soul and skin be of those who have loved the light of your appearing and been drawn to the brightness of your face, who have felt driven to clamber and climb the mountains of our watchful hush until we glimpse your beauty afar and dream of the home to which your Spirit leads us. Through Jesus who loves us and travels our way, Amen.*

Ponder

- What does it mean to you to be a pilgrim? Do you think this is a central aspect of your spiritual identity?
- For what do you hunger in a desperate way? What do you think you'll find on the other side of your hunger?
- What might it mean for God himself to hunger for his people? What does this mean to you, personally?

Part Two

The Shape of Quiet

5

Ox-Cart Man

Limit

When the bright leaves dance in their fall to death, when the air in the mornings is chill, when the days die early in darkness and woodsmoke scents the dampened night, we come in our home to a great event. Marked by the baking of pumpkin bread, the making of strong brewed tea, the culling of quilts and the lighting of crackling fires, we enter the revelry of autumn books. All year they sit high on the picture bookshelf, their beauties reserved for the days of indrawing, when the world outside is wild and wet and we need the grace of their kindling warmth. When they're placed in the basket by the hearth, the festival days of autumn have come. Apples and pumpkins, storm winds and hearthside, each year my children rifle through the stories, stacking the ones they love best in a pile for me to read aloud.

Each year, the first book on the stack is *Ox-Cart Man*.

Set in early colonial America somewhere in New England, the story is almost subversively plain, opening with the lines

"In October he backed his ox into his cart and he and his family filled it up with everything they made or grew all year long that was left over."[1] At first it seems a folksy story, illustrated accordingly by the wondrous Barbara Cooney. The whole of the book is just the account of a farmer, his wife, and their children gathering the fruits of a year of agricultural labor to sell at Portsmouth Market.

But—wool, mittens, candles, turnips, linen—there is a chanted magic, a kind of litany in the way the items are listed. Each item named conjures the world of work that brought it into being so that one feels the ox-cart is laden with the tributary treasures of compact quotidian realms. The book follows the farmer's journey to the market, where he capably sells everything he has, including the cart and the ox that pulled it (with a farewell kiss on the nose). With money in his pockets, the ox-cart man then gathers a few treasures himself, each item a tool to bring greater skill to the crafts of the farm: a new iron pot, a steel embroidery needle, a Barlow knife for carving, and for sheer delight, two pounds of wintergreen candy.

Then home he walks, for ten days, and his first night back sees a simple resumption of the dance and work that produced the earthy riches he has just sold. The final pages follow the family through the year, revealing the slow, daily forms by which the wealth of the farm is made; the planting of gardens, the crafting of a new harness through the snowy days of deep winter, the culling of honey, the tapping of maples, the day by day gathering of the feathers that fall, so slowly, from the geese in the barnyard.

I'm not surprised at my children's choice of this book, because when I was a little one, the very same book held an almost enchanted hold over my imagination. The world it evoked was one of potent and constant creation; I wanted to learn the crafts of the farm. I wanted to fashion and grow things. That story kindled a deep sense of capability in me as I glimpsed a way of life that was fundamentally and lavishly creative even while drawing on the free things of the world: earth and seed, weather and dirt, hard work and goodwill. The story seemed to slow my breath. The cadence and color evoked a deep sense within me of the symphonic nature of ordinary reality. I looked up from its pages to find my own world turning afresh in a kind of dance.

As my world does now in the shadow-bright days when I read this book aloud to my children. I've read it countless times; I can almost recite it from memory. You might think such familiarity would drain the book of the power it wielded over me in child-hood, but instead I find the magic deepened. Each time I read it, the story creates a great quiet in my mind. I find in myself the same old creative itch, the startled sense of a world opening up around me as the trappings of the ordinary are revealed as the stuff of almost enchanted capacity. I'm no farmer, I think, but anybody can plant a garden, yes? Learn a craft?

But the ox-cart man also unsettles me.

This year his story has tangled itself up with all my thoughts about quiet, and I've recognized the larger and far more costly invitation inherent in such a shape of living. On the one hand, it simply images the kind of life, rooted in earth and craft, I think we often crave in our modern lives, severed as we often are from season and soil. But in *Ox-Cart Man* we also stand imaginatively within a world of severe limit. The plenteousness of this man's world is largely enabled by his willing enclosure within the confines of his farm. The generative nature of the life we see in the book proceeds from an almost sacramental and certainly exclusive bond: the marriage of the farmer and his family to this single piece of land, these few apple trees, this undulating field, these seasons, this house, this fellowship of blood and work.

The ox-cart man's life is a truly quiet life, faithful in all the smallest things, and I taste the potent beauty of that as I read to my small, demanding children amidst my small, homebound days. I, too, live in a world of severe limit, but my ease within it is less complete. I am troubled by this book even as I taste its invitation. Each time I've read it this year, with quiet on my mind and wrestling in my heart, two questions have risen, urgent and wild:

Could such a life be enough?

Can I accept such limit?

And I am dismayed in the slowness of my soul's answering.

My life quickened abruptly when I was thirty.

It shocked me; I went from years of waiting for real life to begin to the miracle of an overseas move and new life as a student. As I've written before, the onset of my mental illness at seventeen meant that I missed many earlier openings to independence and vocation. When I finally reached them at age thirty, I wanted only to gain all I had lost in those years of limit. I was abruptly set back in that sphere of almost endless possibility that usually marks late teens. Everything seemed in reach. Within five years, I barreled through two degrees and two book contracts, married the man I'd fallen in love with (who actually loved me too), and welcomed our first child into this new, burgeoning existence. The years of the locusts had been redeemed. I often walked the streets in Oxford feeling I had fallen into some of the impassioned dreams of my youth.

But when I stopped for breath and looked around, I found myself already hungry for the next thing, and at the back of my joy grew a great fear of falling behind. I wanted a third degree, I wanted my books to be published, my voice to be heard, not from a sense of my particular importance but because the hunger still drove me. I still had this sense that significance was out there to be claimed, and I needed to push a little harder to grasp it.

The world agreed with my hunger. Academia seems driven by the ideal of expansion—of knowledge, accomplishment, influence. If you're smart, you should do whatever it takes to make yourself noticeable. So, too, the land of publishing. The internet allows literally boundless possibilities for connection with potential readers. Influence online is a mercurial goddess who strikes and blesses at random but also and at the same time is a power to be harnessed by dogged engagement, by daily post after video after reel. I looked around, and it seemed to me that success meant pushing against all the limits I had learned to abide by in the years of my cloistering. Success and even health seemed bound up in the idea of continual, radical growth.

And for a while, I fretted desperately after that expansion.

When my first child was seven months old, I began a graduate degree in modern theology. I was very naïve, not realizing the extent to which my study of contemporary theology would include nineteenth-century philosophy or how much work would be required for me to grasp these new concepts. I underestimated the tension I would feel between my life as a mother and my life as a student; from the very first seminar, I knew my brain and skin and time were torturously inadequate to all the demands I was setting upon them.

The momentum of my three past years of successful academic work, attained so late, drove me forward with a sense that I had something momentous to accomplish, that the essays lurking in my brain were necessary to the theological conversations of my time. But my heart was also wholly given to my daughter; to this scrap of soul and belovedness I could barely bring myself to leave even for a few hours of study. I swallowed the rising conflict in my heart and body by telling myself that anything is possible, yes? I did not want to be limited by motherhood; I did not want to fade from the world I had just discovered. And fueled still by the pervasive, atmospheric sense around me that the only limit to my accomplishment was myself, I drove forward.

One day, I sat in a rooftop café with late autumn light burning my cheek through the window. I couldn't move because my baby had fallen asleep in the stroller holding my right hand. Very gingerly, with my left, I turned the pages for that week's seminar reading, from the philosophy of Nietzsche. We'd gotten through Kant and Hegel, and though I could trace their influence upon modern theology with some work, my biggest takeaway from both was a grumpy wish that they'd fathered ten children and had less time to write. But Nietzsche, madman and destroyer of faith, fascinated me. His work was twisted and imaginative, truthful and awful and compelling; he understood the motivations and desires of the human heart, and he called out the hypocrisies and self-service that so often ape a life of "faith." And in place of Christianity's ideals of humility and compassion, he posited "the will to power." Fundamental, he said, to human identity is the need to actualize one's inmost self, one's will, to see it work upon the world.

This was a philosophy I recognized.

Follow your heart.
You can be anything you desire.
Reach for the stars and don't let anyone stand in your way.
The only limit upon what you can accomplish is yourself.

I could conjure a dozen clichéd phrases shaping the ideals of contemporary culture that expressed, at heart, Nietzsche's belief that our happiness, the true fulfillment of human endeavor, lies in the kind of self-realization that shatters limit, that asserts its power and potency by overcoming other obstacles and selves.

The problem I suddenly found was how Nietzschean my own ideals of advancement now seemed. The noise of the café grew distant as I began to wonder what voice was at work in the restless battering of my ambition. I recognized his ideals in the nature of my boundless desire, my harried need to prove my worth and claim my place in the world. But it wasn't this that stopped me cold.

It was my daughter's hand as it lay warm and weighted in mine. I closed Nietzsche and checked again to make sure of her breathing under the feather-light blanket. I flexed a muscle, trying to stretch my arm without moving it or waking her. And I felt the chilled calm of a sudden realization.

Whatever power I possessed was yielded to this child, willingly. With the whole of my being, I served her. The full possession of myself—my body, my time, my creativity, my hopes for the future—were things I did not think twice about offering to my child, and this was no means of manipulation. This was gift. Self poured out for the other. This was limit. I could not be any other. And it was one of the best things I had ever experienced.

I sat there realizing that there was little place for motherhood in Nietzsche's philosophy, for the kind of power expressed as affection, as service, as self-gift. There was little room for any kind of power but the dominative, no room for limit or dependence, for the idea of the self as created to be finite, humbly reliant upon a thousand other selves even for existence. I was profoundly aware of my daughter's need of me, and with that awareness came an ever-expanding knowledge of the interwoven nature of human identity and life, a connectedness I realized was integrally at odds with the messages I had been internalizing for months.

What if I couldn't do anything I wanted? What if love for my child, health for my body, or care for my neighbor meant a boundary to what I could desire? Would that mean a Nietzschean descent into the despair of a self unrealized, or was there a different way to understand the significance of a life poured out in small, generous, faithful acts?

A life of limit. Of quiet. A life of love.

In Tobias Wolff's novel *Old School*, there's a scene set in a private American boys' school in the Kennedy era when a class of budding teenage poets has a conversation with the great poet Robert Frost, who is visiting the school to give a special lecture. The boys are precocious, caught up in all the foible and freshness of free verse; they're also suspicious and dismissive of this old man who "still uses rhyme." Until the poet himself confronts them and argues powerfully for the merits of "form" as he speaks about grief:

I am thinking of Achilles' grief, he said. That famous, terrible, grief. Let me tell you boys something. Such grief can only be told in form. Form is everything. Without it you've got nothing but a stubbed-toe cry—sincere, maybe, for what that's worth, but with no depth or carry. No echo. You may have a grievance but you do not have grief, and grievances are for petitions, not poetry.[2]

I think I read those words amidst my year of graduate philosophy and quickly recognized the larger idea that loomed behind them. If poetry means nothing without form, what is life itself, our ordinary days, the larger shape of our reaching? Surely form is as necessary to life as to word, yet what is form in the end but limit—the words we cannot use, the cadence we have to keep, the rhythm we must not lose?

But we hear the word *limit* in much the same way we hear the word *quiet*: as a form of subtraction, a curtailment of what could or ought to be ours. We despise it as old-fashioned, a diminishment of personal freedom, just like those arrogant boys in *Old School*.

But what is freedom to begin with? Something boundless we're born with, innate to human existence? Are we truly free, mired as we are in nurture and inheritance, the strictures of our time, the limits of science? Or is freedom a gift, something we do not own and cannot receive except by generosity?

I did take some mighty good from my graduate year, mostly due to independent research. The main reason I studied modern theology to begin with was a Swiss theologian named Hans Urs von Balthasar, and he was every bit as good as I hoped he would be. Balthasar was a philosopher, priest, and theologian whose work was, in many ways, an answer to the prevailing modern philosophies of his time, Nietzsche's foremost among them. Balthasar understood the compelling nature of Nietzsche's ideas, saw the way they wooed the human sense of identity and significance, saw how they warped the God-breathed hunger for the eternal in the heart of humankind. Of course we desire the world and everything in it; we bear the image of the world-making God.

But our power, wrote Balthasar, unlike God's, is entirely contingent, wholly dependent upon God's permission. Because we are created beings, we can only possess what our Maker gives us. The radical thing is that we have any power at all, that God doesn't abuse our dependency in order to coerce us. Rather, in Balthasar's glowing words, in God we discover "the radiant goodness of absolute freedom, which gives the most precious thing it has."[3]

Further, God himself teaches us how to use this most precious freedom, how to employ this power. Balthasar agrees with Nietzsche that power is at the heart of human identity; freedom is what we crave. But freedom for what? Nietzsche sees freedom as the means by which we impose and establish ourselves in many senses *against* others. Balthasar, radically and beautifully, sees freedom as primarily a form of generosity. In Jesus we discover the ultimate form of freedom in a life lived entirely as gift. In Balthasar's words, God's "absolute power is identical with absolute self-giving."[4] Instead of a power used to coerce and impose, we were made for a power expressed in love, in offering our finite selves, one to another.

Our very embodiment reveals the contours of our severely boundaried nature. We cannot be anything we want. We cannot have everything we desire. We cannot keep up with the internet. We cannot achieve every goal we set or conquer every person just ahead of us. We cannot live like the tireless machines and sleepless screens by which so much of our lives are now enabled and measured. And when we try, it is no wonder that skin and blood, heart and soul begin to fray, to fester, to fail. I think it's no coincidence that an age that despises limit is also the era of skyrocketing rates of anxiety, depression, and loneliness.

At the heart of the striving that decimates quiet in our lives is the voice of the snake in the garden, whispering that limit is an evil thing, a trick. Our hatred of limit is a loss of the fundamental trust that existed between human and Creator in the beginning. Satan has always been against limit and always works to make us think it is a form of divine withholding.

But Love is at the heart of power, as He ought to be, and because of this we live in a paradoxical grace; we are limited beings to whom unlimited love is given. And with that comes endless possibility. There's no such thing as a limitless self, but there is a God who dwells in our hearts, and the freedom of the cosmos is in his hands. We are a poem spoken by God, and, like the fictionalized Frost said, it's in the *forms* of divine affection and creativity, holy forgiveness, and fellowship shown to us in Christ that we'll find the expression of self, the fulfillment of personhood we so desire.

But what does this have to do with quiet?

It's autumn as I write. The cherry tree out the window glints with the first of the burning leaves. Soon the fires of this season will kindle in all the leaves of the country around us, the winds will come, the air will cool, and it will be time to pull out *Ox-Cart Man* again.

Beside me lies a book of poems. I've been reading one or two each morning as a way to start the day in a kind of cadenced attention. One in particular stirs me; I page constantly back to it, often ending my time by yet another skim of its brief, beautiful lines. All day it echoes in my mind, a lilting poem of simple words describing a husband watching his wife cook dinner, watching her taste the sauce, sip her wine, look out the window at the honeyed light. It ends, "we ate, we drank, we went to bed, / It was a miracle."[5]

I glanced at the poet's name when I first read it and thought it looked familiar. It's only been recently, as I readied our stack of autumn books, that I realized its author, Donald Hall, was the very same poet who composed the lyric beauty of *Ox-Cart Man*. Of course I see it now, the same clarity of sight revealing ordinary acts of creativity and love as potent with divine significance.

It was a miracle.

This is where quiet comes in.

We cannot see the world in the way Hall sees it, the way Balthasar sees it, or Christ, or even a little child, if we cannot stand in quiet. Here in the hush and stillness of affectionate attention, we discover, yes, our limits, but in them also a depth we did not suspect in the frenzy of our reaching. From a world held hostage by the idea that the quantifiably big, the numerically great, and the visibly expansive accurately describe our worth, we return to the magic of a world in a grain of sand, the universe compacted in a seed. From an anxious world full of desperate souls trying to impose their agendas and needs, identities, and desires upon every person in their path, we come home to a self whose freedom is a given thing guaranteed not by power but by Love.

To stand in quiet doesn't mean to abandon ambition or desire; I've never lost my need to chase stories or untangle ideas or scratch them both out on paper. I still have a lifetime of things I want to learn. But quiet has taught me to understand those desires as rooted in the self-giving form of the great Love who guarantees my freedom in the first place. My dreams are anchored in the life I've been given by "In October he backed his ox into his cart and he and his family filled it up with everything they made or grew all year long that was left over." God, the fragile body in which those desires grow, the people to whom I am connected by love, the boundaried place in which I both dream and dwell.

Can such a life, then, be enough?

This time I can answer . . . yes.

Pray

O God, whose power is love, whose freedom is given, teach us the grace of being tethered to you. May limit be our gift, the realm in which we live and move and make in the cadence of your grace. May we see our lives as miracles, our days as poems of your making, written in the mighty forms of compassion, of creativity, of joy. Let us know ourselves rich in the wealth of the countless small realms where your Spirit dwells. Make us humble, make us gentle, give us grace to find our lives abundantly enough, through Jesus who gave the whole of himself to make them so, Amen.

Ponder

- What does freedom mean to you? Do you come closer to Nietzsche or Balthasar in your answer?
- Can you call the confines of your life *enough*?
- What might it take for you to understand your own days as "a miracle"?

6

Words Make Worlds

Cadence

O Lord, open thou our lips . . .[1]

Lit candles cheer my jetlagged heart. They frame and cradle the unshaped, lingering dark of the hours before dawn. A traveler might find herself sore-eyed, unraveled in the long night. But the self-assertion of a small, merry flame, defiant of the great dark round it, coaxes my mind into an assertion of its own. And the power of the mind is in the words it kindles, bright and fierce, to shape the night.

And our mouths shall shew forth thy praise . . .

Words, like light, can frame the time and space in which we move. Like flame in a darkened room, words have the power to define and form our hours, to shape the spaces of time in which we relate, create, believe. The words we use to describe and meet each day, the ones we allow to shape the contours of our experience, teach us what to see and how to meet both joy in the day and sorrow in the darkness. Words make worlds, you know, and each one we speak forms the way we see our own.

O God, make speed to save us . . .

So does quiet. Music is formed by the silence between notes, poetry comes in the rest between words, and the quiet spaces in which we root our attention become the cadence to the symphony of the story we are forming day by day. As flame carves the darkness into a shape to bear its brightness, as words make the window through which we see the world, so quiet becomes the great steady heartbeat of a life formed by listening for the God who speaks us free, rather than the unending uproar of a fallen world.

O Lord, make haste to help us . . .

Ten years ago, when I first moved to Oxford, one of the great adventures of my new student season was the chance to take part in the practice of daily, corporate, liturgical prayer. I hadn't realized this would be so available to me, but as a student of theology in an ancient English center of worship, I found myself invited to join daily services of prayer at every turn: in evensongs at college chapels, in daily services at my college, in early morning communion at the church where I worshiped. So, I went. There was a part of me that had always hungered for this kind of immersion. I remember telling my mother once that if I knew how, I'd really love to be pious. I think what I meant is that I yearned for a larger form to my worship, an embodied "scaffolding" to my spiritual life, as I heard one priest describe it in a lecture. This was my chance; morning and evening, I gathered with others to speak and hear spoken the songs, canticles, Scriptures, psalms, and collects said for centuries by those who have worshiped in the Anglican Church.

Glory be to the Father, and to the Son, and to the Holy Ghost . . .

In the mornings, the air was sharp and cold in the chapel, and we shuffled, subdued, into the hush of early day. The words of the prayers fell like drops of water on the cool surface of our sleepy minds, rippling out to wake and gird us for the day. At evening, the shadows clustered like dark birds under the pews, and the air was thick with cold and with our own breath as the prayers for protection rose from our lips while the light failed. The words were a kind of starlight blossoming in the mind.

The Lord Almighty grant us a peaceful night and a perfect end . . .

Quiet. Candlelight. Prayer. These quickly became the set points of my day, and I was surprised by this. I was in a season when essay deadlines and lecture appointments would usually have rendered me oblivious to the passage of time or the keeping of devotions; I knew I'd usually be up all hours with little time set aside for rest. Instead, I found myself drawn into an alternate rhythm that protected a space of peaceful quiet each day. Right before the Christmas break, I asked a tutor a few of my growing questions about the Book of Common Prayer (the liturgy we all used) and how to engage it on my own during my weeks away. He rummaged in a cupboard that looked like it had been there since the book was first composed (in 1549) and emerged with a copy that didn't look much younger. He apologized that it was the only one he had to hand, with its battered maroon cover and tattered seams. But I liked its age. It meant other hands than mine had loved it. "Read this," he said. "Study it, use it now and then in your devotions, and you will understand a lot simply by way of worship."

Into thy hands, O Lord, I commend my spirit . . .

So I did. I kept it on the windowsill next to my bed during my final essays, and I began to say the confessions at night, the psalms and collects early in the morning. And then I took it home with me, back to the States, for Christmas break. In the strange airplane twilight, that void and formless space between places and times that has always kindled anxiety in me, I opened that battered little book and found that the words wove round me, the quiet cradled me, and the day began in peace. When jetlag woke me in the wee sma's, and night thoughts began their anxious spin, I said the old compline liturgies, asking for protection and light. And I found it.

For thou hast redeemed me, O Lord, thou God of truth . . .

I think it was in those first weeks home, away from the rhythms of my Oxford life, that I realized how great was the gift of that prayerful cadence, how much it had formed and rested me in so short a time. To kneel, to breathe deeply, to let quiet settle round me as I prepared myself to speak the first words of the liturgy had become an almost physical space of refuge, as if I could draw a tent round myself for a few minutes, a few moments that rooted all the rest of my day in a sense of surety. I understood that I had begun something with the power to deeply shape the rest of my life. I was raised in a home that gave me the inestimable habit of a daily quiet time; this only built upon that rich foundation. But the special gift it offered was a shape and a language that did not depend upon my inclination or emotion. Especially back in Oxford, when the times for prayer were set services and my physical presence was required at a particular dot on the clock, I found myself formed to and by something greater than me, by words I did not write, by hush I did not conjure but join.

Keep me as the apple of an eye . . .

I was intrigued, and when I got back to my studies in England, I began to formally study the way liturgy and ritual shape our experience of time. I studied the Celtic church, for I had always been attracted by the beauty of my Celtic Daily Prayer book, my first taste of morning and evening prayer. I found that the early Celtic Christians understood all of time, including the ordinary time of daily work and rest, as participating in eternity. Their formal liturgies and prayers were points of contact with the larger story of Christ's invasion of time, the space in which they wove mystery with mundanity and made all of it worship. Time was a story redeemed, one that was broken by the fall but drawn back into epic, narrative goodness by the life of Christ. Each feast, each liturgy, each ritual reflected that reality and wove the believer who kept them into the healing story Jesus told with his own embodied life, one to which every believer is invited.

Hide me under the shadow of your wings . . .

I realized, then, how formless our own experience of time is in the twenty-first century, untethered not just from prayer but from sun or moon, season or tide. The internet never sleeps, electricity means that darkness need not halt work, and we are too worldly wise and weary to shape our days by any great story. I sat that year in a series of lectures given by a hospital chaplain who told us we were one of the first civilizations in history to have no liturgy for death. Unlike medieval Christians, who wrote literal guides to dying well in times of plague, we moderns have no story to comfort our passing, no shape or language of ritual or liturgy by which to traverse the darkness of loss. Of course, Christians of all kinds carry the hope of the resurrection with them, but what shape does that hope take? What are the words by which it may be grasped, the shape by which it may be felt as the taste-and-see goodness of God in the face of our unraveling?

Preserve us, O Lord, while waking . . .

If pain is visceral, so must our prayer be. We need not just the abstract words of petition but a way to embody and enact our desire, a form by which we may ask for the comfort of our Savior and dwell in the companionship of the saints. We need words that weave a refuge about us in the battered world in which we pray.

And guard us while sleeping . . .

It's been ten years since my first wondrous autumn of prayerful exploration. But the study and wonder I found in that first year has shaped the whole of my spiritual life since (not least because it was at an evening service that I first saw my future husband by candlelight). On a sheerly pragmatic level, I am now the wife of a priest who leaves each morning to lead the very same liturgy of morning prayer that first so stirred and kindled me in Oxford. I'm counting the days until my children are old enough to join; when they do, I will teach them to kneel when the prayers begin, to gather body and heart into a physical form of attention. I'll teach them to speak the daily liturgies—mostly just Scripture put to cadence—in conscious company with Christians around the world through countless years. My husband and I, we're old-fashioned, with his work rooted in a little church that believes in the ancient cadences. I love that my children will experience the rhythm of daily prayers and personal devotion as well as yearly feasts, our family life revolving round these high days and holy, ordinary moments.

That awake we may watch with Christ, and asleep we may rest in peace . . .

But I also love that we will be shaped, as I am daily challenged, to the kind of life in which such prayer is possible, and that is a life of cultivated quiet. Quiet planted and tended like a garden, watched and guarded. Quiet is not an abstract thing we can pull down from the air but the formation of habit and time, a claiming of physical shapes and daily spaces. Quiet is not an idea but a form we choose and staunchly inhabit. I think prayer is the great language of quiet, but I learned it by entering the hushed space that daily prayer allowed me, the watchful, holy spaces of the quiet that roots and precedes corporate worship.

Christ have mercy upon us . . .

What does that mean? I'm still working it out ten years on. But as I have explored the realm and reality of living in quiet, I have learned to ask myself these questions:

What are the shapes of quiet?

What are its cadences?

How may I so frame the time I am given each day that quiet is claimed as a holy space, cupped so I may sip from its nourishment?

Asking these questions has helped me to move away from an idea of quiet as something primarily about negation—subtracting people (a near impossibility with four small children in the house), noise, and activity from my life—to something that is claimed or created. To a positive thing I craft by shaping the hours I have been given, understanding them not as neutral space but rather the soil of my life out of which will grow whatever I choose to plant in the loamy earth of my given days. My experience of liturgy, cadence, and ritual, of time shaped by worship, has been vital to me.

Give peace, O Lord, in all the world . . .

As I have walked this prayerful way, asking those haunting questions, I've found an understanding of sacramental vision to be indispensable to my work. Back in my student days, I accepted the invitation of a priest to ask any question I had about the liturgical worship I was just beginning to enter. I showed up at his door the next week with a piece of paper covered on both sides with questions. We sat down with the Bible, the Book of Common Prayer, and a book called *Heavenly Participation* by Hans Boersma. The first thing the priest explained was the idea of sacramentality. This is "the outward and visible sign of an inward and spiritual grace."[2] Usually, this refers to things like receiving the Eucharist, baptism, or marriage, outward rituals that make a spiritual reality visible. But once one understands the nature of a sacramental life, one begins to grasp that the whole of the world is sacramental by design, meant to be for us the sign and presence of God's beauty, his goodness, his care. Nature is no mere gathering of atoms but rather the outward form of God's imagination. Our bodies aren't peripheral to our faith but intimately bound up in the outworking of redemption. Time isn't neutral but rather the space in which God's story is told anew, renewed, restarted by the historic arrival of Jesus.

I found this quote by Boersma and have pondered it often:

> Augustine's concept of time was sacramental: time participates in the eternity of God's life, and it is this participation that is able to gather past, present, and future together into one.[3]

These words have helped me to understand that in creating spaces of quiet—whether by joining those crafted by the larger worshiping church or claiming them in the smaller drama of my own days—I am enacting and inhabiting God's story. When I choose to shape the hours of my life in such a way that they become the space in which I listen for God's voice and expect his arrival, I am entering the Christian way of understanding time as redeemed from a fallen cascade into disaster by the arrival of God himself in the circles of our embodied days.

O Lord, save thy people and bless thine heritage . . .

Day by day, year by year, I am learning to live increasingly in a life cadenced by quiet. At the most basic, and when I am not too tired to keep it, for me this has meant setting anchors of quiet as the opening to my morning and the closing to my day. Before phone or screen, before even entering the jolly uproar of breakfast and family, I try to take a few minutes of silence. I am not in a season when I may attend regular services of prayer in a church setting (even though the church is across from my house). I'm not even in a season when I can get up very early, what with the nightly habits of my youngest. But I can, most days, sit in the chair I've set by my window. Open it so the freshened chill of morning bathes my face. I can breathe and remember the breath and kindness of God who holds me in life. I can read a poem. I can open my Bible, even if it's to read a single verse. I can let the great quiet of that space begin to breathe in me, and when the words rise, I can pray. I can keep a prayer book next to my chair with a simple morning blessing that is manageable most days.

Same for the evening. My rhythms here change; it is sometimes a few words of thanks jotted in a journal, sometimes a snippet of Evening Prayer, sometimes a choral song played into the shadows, sometimes the mere choice to breathe long and deep for a few minutes before turning to my novel and to sleep.

Lighten our darkness, we beseech Thee, O Lord . . .

One thing I've learned: quiet resides in our skin and bones as well as in our minds, and one cannot claim time for Christ without also claiming the physical experience and space that allow it. We need sleep. We need the breath of God's Spirit that comes in prayer and deeper breath for our lungs. We need spaces even in our homes that affect us in the same way as the ancient hush of an old church, its stone walls soaked in prayer. So I think about the corners where quiet will reign in my home. I set little spaces where the children or I can be alone to read or think. I light many candles, for there is a kind of sacramental grace in their small, flamed light, casting their circles of sheltered brightness.

And by Thy great goodness, defend us against all fears and enemies this night . . .

There is a storied nature to this work, this daily shaping of quiet, this transformation of ordinary spaces by the simple disciplines of attention and prayer. We live in a fallen world where space and time are often just the place where bad things happen and good things slowly fade. This is an age of nihilism, in which the constant reality of war and horror has left many with a profound sense that there is no meaning to our actions, our days, the pouring out of our lives within the random chances of this world. To live in such a way that our hours are tethered to the tale of Christ is to live a redemptive narrative with the whole of our lives. In the holy quiet we claim, God's goodness sings afresh for a broken world.

For the love of Thy only Son, our Savior, Jesus Christ.

As I write, I'm in that strange space of advent as I await the arrival of our fourth child. My belly is big, my movements slow. Quiet gathers round me as rest becomes not a choice among many but the one thing needed. I sit in my room most days as I wait. I'm trying to watch and ponder in a different way than I have before. I know that once this little one is born, the whole of myself will want to rush into the movement and productivity I've lacked for months. I know the urge I will feel to prove myself strong and able after a season of feeling profoundly weak in the pouring out of my body for that of my child. But I also know that to rush the early days of infancy is to miss a sacred space of profound quiet in which I may meet the soul and body of my child. I'm trying, this time, to prepare the spaces of the days after the birth to be a time of cradling and attention. Candles, books, quiet music, the soft blankets we'll need for warmth in the October cold of this old house; each day, I gather these outward signs of the love I bear for my child, the tangible embodiment of the peace and hush in which I want her life to open. I am telling the story of her preciousness by the quiet I am preparing for us to enter upon her birth.

Glory be to the Father, the Son, and the Holy Ghost.

But I hope that story extends into all the spaces of my life. I want the shape of my living to cry out in witness to the coming of God as I craft the spaces of quiet, choosing every day the rhythms and shapes by which I may receive his actual goodness at work in the story of my life. The shape of quiet, for me, is the shape of my watchful gratitude as he comes.

As it was in the beginning, is now, and shall be forever. Amen.

Pray

O God, from whose bright words the world was formed, speak us now into healed and hearty life. Show us the shapes of love by which we may form our hours; teach us the lines of prayer by which we may speak your story. Help us to live a life of shapely grace, of tangible hope, of enacted faith. Lead us, word by word and hour by hour, into the cadence of praise that makes for a life that tells the joy of your coming. Let us hunger and trust, worship and sing, in the great, graced quiet of your love, through Jesus whose heart beats in ours, Amen.

Ponder

- What does it mean for quiet to have a shape or a cadence? What words or acts could give it a tangible presence for you?
- Consider: How might liturgy and cadence, set words for prayer, allow you to step into a space of quiet or attention?
- What does it mean to you for time to be shaped in such a way that it tells a story?

7

Color of Wonder

Prayer

The light pulls me from sleep; the blue light blurs the edges of the waking world pressing in at my window, allowing me a few merciful minutes between the hard reality of rising and the dim, soft world of my lost sleep.

I catch at quiet, then, first thing. It's like the light, untouchable but potently there in that fragile moment, and I try to turn my heart to greet the silence, to soak myself in its presence. For just that moment, the day lies unformed before me, and my heart rises to meet the possibility. I try to pray. *Hear, O Israel*; I remember the words the Jews have spoken for centuries every day, the prayer said first thing in the light of the new morning. Before you dress or eat or move, hear, people of God, attend and remember who it is who set your soul afire and your body alight.

For many years now, I have yearned daily toward this discipline. I shall set myself alert. I, too, shall attend and lift up my heart. I begin to inwardly pray the words from the Celtic Daily Prayer book I've used for years:

> One thing I have asked of the Lord, this I shall seek, that I may dwell in the house forever.

But just as I begin to imagine what dwelling in the house and presence of God might mean, the toddler who has been cuddled in my arms since the small hours wakes suddenly and butts my shoulder with her tousled head. And though the quiet is not gone nor my prayer done, I turn from it to her, and to the chorus of other voices that tug me into the gathering rapids of the day. I tumble forward.

Has the world always been such a mad dash and so busy, or is something just wrong with me? I mull this question almost every day as I putter between bedroom and bathroom and children. The problem is not actually the happy fuss of four small children and two parents with work to do and ministry to offer and yearning and grief of their own. That's just the way of things. Countless households through the centuries have been wilder than mine, and though I sometimes dream toward a country life, I don't imagine waking on a farm is any calmer than waking in the city.

But it's not the outer disquiet that troubles me. It's the inward one; the buzz of frenzy round the edges, the latent disquiet of my mind that disturbs me and has been the subject of my contemplation for any number of years now. The older I've gotten, the fuller my life, the more I'm aware that the patterns of the world around me drain and exhaust the deep spaces of my soul. I go to bed with a mind still frenzied by a scroll through the internet. I wake too often with a psyche exhausted, feeling that something essential is missing, that something vital has escaped me; and from the moment I wake, I am running to catch it.

Which makes real prayer a rather elusive thing.

What is it with the modern world? I wonder if I am simply undisciplined. Or is it that I have exchanged the finite rhythms of the earth for the limitless stare of the internet? I can feel my phone brooding in the corner of my study where I firmly put it away last night. I feel the glare of its eye as I move about the hall upstairs, six small feet pattering in my wake. I've told myself I will not look at a screen before I've prayed, before I've done something to root myself in some sense of God's reality each day. But I'm already tired after a night up with my babe, and the impulse to see who's texted, what interesting thing has happened, what new disaster looms, what opinion has broken wild and fiery upon the world, is an itch that is damnably hard not to scratch. So I turn, almost desperate, to dress my children.

Lord, have mercy, I breathe. *Please.* Long ago I read a novel about a woman with a wretched mental illness on the verge of a breakdown who encountered an old priest in a garden. He spotted her misery and asked her if she knew how to pray. She balked, a little offended at the thought of prayer to the God who would allow her disease. But he, with decades of clinical depression under his belt, was unperturbed:

> There are three necessary prayers, and they have three words each. They are these, "Lord have mercy. Thee I adore. Into Thy hands." Not difficult to remember. If in times of distress you hold to these, you will do well.[1]

Better, anyway. Those prayers are surprisingly potent. So, *Lord have mercy*, I breathe again and pour myself into the day.

Our house is a big, drafty, gorgeous Victorian-era vicarage in England that comes with my husband's job as a priest. There's no heating the thing efficiently, especially now as autumn burnishes the leaves and the chill soaks into the wood floors and beautifully molded corners. But the house is filled with the special kind of light that filters through paned, leaded glass—the old, fragile kind. Every room has many-paned windows, and in the mornings the sunlight spills through them like diamonds. I walk the hall all shivery and cold but newly awake, slipping in and out of the shafts of thick, silvered light, lifting my eyes to it as I pass from room to room, the silent brilliance a kind of invitation. As I walk, praying for mercy, I can feel something deepening in myself, feel my spirit reaching out toward that light, toward the way it draws eye and soul into its quiet, and something deep within my heart rises hungering.

O Lord, open thou my lips . . .

But time is galloping ahead, and I cannot stop. I'm dressed and downstairs at the kitchen counter, coffee clutched gratefully, before I realize that yet again in the rush to be downstairs before my husband's departure, I've forgotten to say my two minutes of prayer or read my daily psalm. My phone sits in my hand; I've been surreptitiously scrolling Instagram in between buttering many pieces of toast, and I sigh, and for a moment I feel profoundly unraveled. This small habit, to say my prayers before I look at my phone, seems both tiny and mighty, a small thing to do and a work sometimes laughably beyond my grasp. I can feel frustration rise in me, the kind that drains the world of its color. How will I ever grow, ever find God in all the madness of the world if I cannot make myself do this one thing?

I sigh again. The toast is getting cold.

But my three small souls are all in a chatter about the robin out the window, and my delight is needed to make their observations complete. I join them, dully, crouching on my knees to look with them out the panes of the kitchen door to where a brave, cheeky little bird is hopping ever closer in hope of a crumb. English robins are tiny fairy creatures, very different from their plump American cousins. This one seems intent upon charming us, cocking its head, wings in a whirred dance. Part of me feels profoundly detached from this moment, mired still in an abstract place of frustration, but the sudden belly laugh of my son startles me awake. Abruptly, I remember Robert Louis Stevenson's whimsical but reckless poem requesting God to waken his dulled, bored soul by "stabbing his spirit broad awake."[2]

I am stabbed—and healed—by the laughter of my child. And for a moment, quiet grows up around me, not a quiet that is a detraction of noise or subtraction of all the wrong things I've done but one that is the distillation of attention. In a moment that seems to linger outside of time, that stretches to bear the weight of my sudden focus, I witness the awe of my children, watch their fascination with this workaday bird, noses pressed against the glass panes. Their screeches, their laughter are unconscious thanks for the simple fact of their being.

This, I think, is quiet.

In that moment all the furor of my mind falls away, and I am rooted in a sense of God's benevolence. For an instant, I feel as if I could turn around and feel God, too, kneeling behind me, laughing at the robin. Such moments, they are so fleet. But their grace is an unceasing invitation to turn and try once again, to reach toward the real, to find, at the heart of my dusty old life, a love that makes all small things precious.

This, I think, is also prayer, as I turn my attention once more to the great inward light that is God's presence, a light undimmed by my frailty or the frenzy of the world. *Reorientation* means to turn literally toward the east where the sun will always rise, so I reorient my heart to the dawn of God's presence within me. *Thank you.* It's all the prayer I can manage, but in this moment, it is enough.

What *is* daily, interior prayer?

And how in the world does one become good at it?

Quiet, for me, is at the heart of that question, and prayer is the language of quiet.

Quiet seems to be that natural condition in which I am able to begin that inward attention, that gathering and offering of myself to God that is what I understand prayer to be. I know there are many other kinds of prayer to be explored: prayer in community, prayers of liturgy, prayers of intercession. But I suppose what I chase in these questions is prayer as that inward, daily, individual conversation with my Maker.

For many years, in my long thinking about the relationship between prayer and quiet, I think the definition I would have given to *quiet* was just . . . silence. Prolonged silence attended by undisturbed solitude. This fit with so much of the literature I was reading about interior prayer, the progression of the mystic way, the need to be deeply still. I have always been drawn to contemplative writing, to the interior life, to this sense of burrowing so far into the quiet that one finds God's voice more . . . audible? Understandable? Reachable? Silence was something much more abundantly possible to me as a younger woman. Driven by a deep desire for a keener sense of God's presence, an echo of his voice, I often spent long hours trying to become one of the contemplatives I so admired.

It was worthy work, and it certainly bore fruit in my life as I learned to walk in a kind of companionship with God, turning my thoughts back to him throughout the day. I can honestly say that I did encounter God's goodness and presence in those seasons—sometimes. There was no equation for it, no set number of actions or fixed amount of silence whose combination equaled a mystical encounter. But there was, in myself, an increasing rootedness, a deep sense of walking in company with my Maker.

But if prayer equals silence, then it's something no longer available to me. Nor, really, is it possible to countless people around the world whose lives have no space for leisure or solitude. When I began university at thirty and when I married my husband, the spaces of my life vastly changed, and it took me a long time to figure out what it looked like for me to continue my spiritual life in the presence both of an "other" and of good, demanding work. My husband and I were now always together, a companionship I had deeply craved but one that also meant I had to relearn the patterns of my devotion within the shared spaces of our lives. I now worked, and have since, largely on deadlines.

I was hammering this out amidst the intensity of finishing my degree when our daughter joined us, and quiet, let alone solitude, became something as rare as the proverbial blue moon. I struggled mightily with a sense that, in the entanglement of new marriage and work and motherhood, I had somehow obscured or even harmed the inward spiritual life that had defined and shaped me until that time. Without the trappings of what I thought prayer should include—focus, rest, solitude, silence—I felt that I was not praying, and I labored long and guiltily under a feeling that someday, when I was more disciplined and ordered, I would finally return to the patterns of prayer that made my spiritual life feel valid and real.

In many ways, this was the state of mind in which I began the long mulling of this book. I thought, in those early days, that I would figure out new patterns of discipline by which I could maintain the intensity of focus, reclaim the spaces of silence by sheer discipline. I wonder if most of us approach quiet and prayer in this state, with a pervasive awareness of all the ways we've failed and a bewildered determination to do better. I brought this inward sense of guilt and yearning to my spiritual director one day when my daughter was just over a year old. I expected him to agree with me, to help me wrestle out how to get hold of the discipline that eluded my exhausted mind in that season.

Instead, he astonished me by his immediate and easy assumption that the prayer life I'd known had entirely and permanently departed, right along with the single woman who'd possessed it. It took me a few minutes to digest that, during which time he plunged into an exploration of baby step practices to help me discover the contours of a new, different, developing life of prayer fitted to the need and demand of my current season. I think I finally began to take notes with a raised eyebrow as he fired off a list of practical, tiny, hysterical little ways to tether my wandering attention throughout the day. I felt like a child again, given minuscule assignments: memorize a prayer, write lines, pick five minutes a day for focus. There was nothing beyond the capacity of a child on that list. But one suggestion made me laugh aloud in amusement: pick a color, and every time you see that color, turn your heart to God. Pay attention to his goodness in the smallest things around you.

I walked home with a heart that was both lightened and a little skeptical. The guilt I felt had fallen away for a few minutes . . . but should I let it? Could a life of communion with God really be adequately nourished by such small, ordinary attentions, moments snatched from the furor and rush of daily life? I looked up at the trees lining the cobbled street I walked. *Green.* If I chose green for a day, stepping outside would be an immersion in prayer, grass and leaf, vine and flower. *Blue?* The sky arcs with goodness; I wouldn't be able to look out a window or walk out the door without a startled remembrance of the sapphire love under which we draw breath.

A sweet chill rose on my skin. What if the life of prayer, the rootedness of quiet, was fueled not by discipline but by wonder? What if it was, both in seasons of solitude and seasons of demand, not my grit God mostly wanted but simply my attention?

White . . . like my baby's belly when I kiss it in wondering gratitude for the gift of her. *Red* . . . like the flit of a robin, its presence a whimsical portent, a funny, divine little messenger— and the flushed faces of my children laughing at the gift of it, and the pulse of the blood in my heart as it rises in an unexpected ache of gratitude . . .

I begin to see.

Children know. Sometimes I think the whole form of their little lives is a kind of prayer, and that's what Jesus meant about becoming like a child in order to enter the kingdom. They watch intensely. They notice, and until they have voiced the full extent of their observations and had them validated, they are not to be swayed to another subject. They quest, and they thoroughly question the people they trust. They wonder. Sometimes, in our age of oversaturated opinion, it seems almost too commonplace a thing to say that children possess a capacity for fixed, receptive wonder that their adults have lost, but it's true. It's true. They walk outside in their smallness, and what they see is a kind of workaday miracle, not in the sentimental terms we adults often employ but simply something to be engaged by amazement. Leaves! Airplanes! Wind! Can I taste, touch, join this wildness pouring into the open portals of my whole sensing self?

What is this but the abandoned sort of prayer we all crave?

Poets know too. They understand the way attention can be distilled by the tracing of words until, however briefly, it is pure. Poets have a capacity to listen and wait that I think would serve every lover of God in the life of prayer. The best ones write from their encounter with the wondrous, and oh, they attend: to the quality of what they have witnessed, to the words that might give their encounter accurate and elegant form, to the meter, the rests, that give tongue to the wild and wondrous things they have known.

For the past few years, I have made reading a poem one of those child-sized habits to start my mornings. The words arrest me; they operate almost as the doorway into a different room of attention. When I stand in the space to which they lead me, I find the great hush preceding prayer, not always a long or eloquent prayer but that state of heart in which all things are drawn into conversation with my Maker once more.

Some people are called to the life of intensive silence, of prayer as an expansive vocation of hours and days. Some people find that such prayer attends different seasons of their lives. I lean on the prayers of such people, on their fixity and endurance. They offer up the work of a particular kind of attention that witnesses to one radical way to know and love God. But that is not the only kind of prayer, nor is it the only way to enter a radical orientation to the presence of God and the gifts of quiet. Both lives, the cloistered and silent, the active and noisy, may bear the devotional quality of a life in which prayer is offered up as a constant, interior conversation to the God who orchestrates the dance of relationship and activity, service and feast, parenthood and poetry.

If we define a life of prayer as one measured only by the subtraction of relationship, service, and creativity, then we will think prayer is something we cannot attain and ought not try for. But prayer is that inmost communion with God that roots and nourishes the entirety of our lives. Prayer is an inward conversation, the yielding of all things we find in the tumble of our days to the God who orders and holds them fast. We need its rooting as surely as the mystics, however different the vocations and expressions such prayer fuels. Brother Lawrence, that humble monk who found God in the washing of dishes, once said that "the least little remembrance will always be the most pleasing to Him. One need not cry out very loudly; He is nearer to us than we think."[3]

––––––––

The children are in bed, and I slip out for a walk as the autumn sun sets. The furor of the day still rattles within my mind, but I've left my phone at home; I've set my breath and body and heart for quiet. The walking helps, my blood pounding louder than my thoughts. The cool air helps, summoning me to attention. And the beauty, it is salve and healing, a loveliness that tangles my sight and draws me further up and farther into its hush. The leaves on the trees are now half gold and they flicker; they are like small flames on the branches of the trees that stretch over the darkling water. They rest in small constellations on the surface of the lake, and the ducks float sleepily among them.

What is prayer to me these days among the trappings of children and kitchens and endless conversation? Increasingly I find it grows in me as attention to the One I love. I listen for the beat of his heart at the back of all my work; I watch for his presence to flicker among the pots and pans, the glimmer in a child's eye, the laughter when I snatch my five minutes of reading. His presence, here. Neither earned nor conjured but sought, sought, turned to like a flower to the sun without whose light it will not survive.

The question of prayer, to me, is no longer how I might get enough time or discipline to do "it" but rather, will I turn, in each instance of restored consciousness, returning memory, the whole of myself, to the God who loves me? Will I, like my tiny children, walk abroad in the wildness of the world and turn each question to the One my heart trusts, reach for his hand in the fronting of every experience, shout my thanks, and chuckle my amazement?

I pound across the old wooden bridge over the lake, then climb the steps to the second bridge that stretches over the railway tracks. A half moon, thick and edged like a disk of hard gold, has cut through the sky, and I walk in the light of its laughter as it glimmers through the gently swaying trees. I'm in the woods now, branches tangled and dim all around me, and I stop at the zenith of another bridge, a small wooden one that stretches over a stream choked with lilies and duckweed. A bat dashes across the twilit sky. A star pierces the dark. And I breathe. I'm too tired to muster many words, but I know this quiet, this deep hush is a gift I did not make and cannot claw to myself. I watch. I am full of wonder. And as I stand there, amidst the world shouted into being by the first Word spoken into our hush, as I listen to the beat of love behind the woven song of the trees and stars and sky, I find the birdlike wonder, the robin-sized flutter of joy in my heart, and the words of an old hymn I love rise in the silence:

> Vainly we offer each ample oblation,
> vainly with gifts would his favor secure.
> Richer by far is the heart's adoration,
> dearer to God are the prayers of the poor.[4]

Thank goodness, I think, as the night birds sing.

Prayer

O God, let us revel like children in the rainbow glimmer of your goodness as it glints in our days. Let us count nothing as too small for praise or prayer; no splinter of grief, no sliver of amazement. Catch us with your kindness in all the tiny spaces of silence that fall between our busy hours. Give us a child's grace to find prayer in all its color and love and in all its shapes, through Jesus, the Lord who haunts and hallows each corner of our lives, Amen.

Ponder

- What do you think it means to pray? Do you have a set idea of the conditions or length or what might be accomplished?

- What might it mean for prayer to be not a list of petitions but rather an interior conversation?
- Choose a color for a day and let each sighting of it turn you back to inner and prayerful attention. What do you find?

8

Halcyon Day

Rest

One long-ago day, deep in autumn, when my brother was a student in Boston and I was roaming the country in my little blue hatchback, aching for something to root a self that felt most often shaped like a question mark, I spent a day walking Walden Pond with my brother. We met up near my digs at the end of the Boston train line early in the morning. We'd planned a long walking tour of the Boston streets, a sweeping take of the sights. But we were both silent and bleary-eyed with exhaustion; him with finals, me with the burning of all my existential questions and red-eyed hours of driving. We sat for a few minutes in my car, looking down the barrel of a day for which neither of us had much taste.

"Let's just go to Concord," I said. I remembered this nearby little town fondly from ten years before when we'd visited, in high school, this place where the American Revolution suppos-edly began. But honestly, of more interest to me, it was where

115

Louisa May Alcott, Henry David Thoreau, and Ralph Waldo Emerson all lived in a tangled history of village life and tortured ideals and taut, gleaming words. I knew at least we'd find a café and some shorter walks there.

So we began to drive, and we mostly talked about how tired we were. We must have put on some music, something classical, as we slipped off the highway and onto the backroads. And slowly, slowly, as the furor of the busy day we'd planned faded from our minds, as the woods gathered close to the windows, autumn woods with maple trees like bonfires amidst shadow-woven pines, a larger breath entered our bodies.

I know well from a history of panic attacks that shallow, quickened breath is a symptom of deep distress. I also know well the wild relief that comes when oxygen is suddenly graspable again, when the heart slows and fear recedes and breath, like water, can be deeply drawn. What I didn't know so well until that day is that one can spend months with breath growing shallower each sunrise, until heart and mind race almost at the pace of panic without one ever noticing. Until the grace of a single deep breath. It's like forgiveness. The world starts over.

We inhaled that kind of grace as we entered Concord, parked along the street, and entered a little bakery café. I remember that day in sensory detail that stands out from all the days before it, as if that slowing of breath and mind allowed me to receive the full potency of the tangible world around me. The bakery was tiny and spare, but a row of beautiful old Blue Willow platters lined a high ledge over its counter. They brewed good, strong coffee, which we took away to drink as we walked, and at the last moment I bought us each a flaky cherry and chocolate rugelach from a big, clear jar on the counter. We stepped into crisp air with the high, clean light of a blue-skied autumn day shimmering through the leaves. I felt the woven closeness of my dusk-colorful scarf and its appropriateness to the morning, and I kicked the bright leaves with old boots as we walked down the pavement.

We visited Orchard House first, home of Louisa May Alcott, author of the beloved *Little Women* whose stories shaped my childhood. The house still bore the old paintings she and her sisters made on the walls, the clutter of papers and books not too altered from how she and her idealistic family might have left them. Having always felt a kinship with Jo, the author in the fictional March family, I drew the same sudden thrill of energy I'd taken at sixteen when last I was in this house. I had the sense of being in a place where words formed a world that changed the lives of all who entered it. Here, in these rooms, in the rounds of these ordinary days, a matchless story had been crafted. At the mention of Alcott's admiration for one of her teachers, the famed Henry David Thoreau, Joel and I then decided to take a long ramble around nearby Walden Pond, where Thoreau built his cabin and wrote about a life of nature, solitude, and profound attention.

We needed a picnic first, though, and stopped at a village shop with teetering shelves, buckled wooden floors, and entirely local produce. We got butter and Havarti cheese, apples and ginger beer and a crisp baguette, and we toted it all down to the shores of the pond. We sat on the ledge of an old stone wall and ate very slowly, watching high, threaded clouds unfurl across the sky. We finished, the silence growing happily around and between us as all the beauty of that unexpected hush began to sing into our weariness.

And so began a halcyon day.

One comes across that phrase in old books; it always means a spate of time marked by happiness and peace. The word *halcyon* comes from a Greek tale by Ovid recounting the tragic deaths of Ceyx, son of the morning star, and his wife, Alcyone. So great and beautiful was their love that the gods took pity upon them, reviving both and transforming them into "halcyon birds," or kingfishers. Technically, the halcyon days of this story happen every year in the two weeks surrounding the winter solstice, as Alcyone's father, god of the winds, calms the storms so that his kingfisher daughter may lay her precious eggs upon a gentle sea. But halcyon days have come to mean any time when life and joy stem the tides of suffering; they are a season when no storms rage and the winds blow gentle, when love returns and life begins.

We walked, how long I don't even know. We just began to wander, not at the clipped pace of sightseers or with the stomp of those who come for a single destination. We just . . . ambled. And the maples were like the burning bush when God spoke to Moses, brushing our skin and eyes with a brightness that caused no pain and spoke to us in divine mutterings that stirred us with desire. The pine wood opened its secretive branches so that we trod a dappled path starred by silver coins of birch and oak leaves veined with gold. The pond was emerald in the shadows and sapphire in the sunlight, with rafts of gemmed leaves cresting its miniature waves. A loon observed us, as we did it, from a little alcove of shaded water. The light grew low and the shadows longer as we walked. We watched the branches of the trees become an intricate black lace above us, netting a sky of palest gold. We walked, and we breathed, in quiet.

Later that night, we slipped past the workday traffic back into Boston for a late bowl of chowder at a favorite local café. Afterward, we walked down to Boston Harbor, where the churn and spectacle of the day had receded and a full moon rose mightily over the waters.

We talked about beauty. I think that was one of the first times I consciously articulated the power of beauty to counter and restore destruction, because something deep within me had been healed, abruptly, by that gracious day. I looked on the world around me with what poet Edna St. Vincent Millay calls "quiet eyes,"[1] eyes that could receive my existence as gift. It had been a long time since I was capable of feeling the sheer grace of what it is to draw breath in a God-crafted world. The suffering I had known in mental illness, the anguished years of loneliness, the sense of being lost, lost, obscured by a world where everyone else had a place to belong, a work to accomplish, had embittered my sight. I had raced a little madly down all those road-tripping highways because I had not been able to call my life or story good for a long while, and I was chasing a satisfaction I could not find.

But we also talked about rest, and with it, gift.

Alexander Schmemann, the beloved Russian Orthodox priest and theologian writing in America in the turmoil of the sixties, said that "all that exists is God's gift to man, and it all exists to make God known to man, to make man's life communion with God. It is divine love made food."[2]

On that halcyon day, something essential was returned to me: the knowledge that a fundamental generosity was at work in the crafted beauty of the cosmos and even in my frustrated self. Part of my bitterness was a sense that if I could just do the right thing and choose the right job, or person, or work, I would finally move beyond my loneliness, my need. I was so afraid, so afraid. Of isolation, of a life obscured by suffering and hidden from those who might love or help me. My breath, for months, had been the quickened inhalation of existential panic as I gazed upon my frailty and knew how it curbed and limited my future. I did not reckon upon any strength but my own, and I knew it would fail me.

But in the widened space, the deepened breath, the gathered quiet of that halcyon day, I came home to a place of recollected trust.

The Christian mystics often use the term *recollection*. It's an old-fashioned word for *memory*, in whose meaning it partakes. The online New Advent Encyclopedia, like several others, defines it as "attention to the presence of God in the soul."[3] Usually it involves a turning away from outward things to the inmost things, to a place of silence where we may become aware of God's presence constantly breathing in and through us.

But I have come to believe strongly that the startled quiet, the focused attention conjured in us by an encounter with the benevolence of even the outer world of creation, is a way of walking to this inward place. At the heart of recollection is a return to the knowledge of our origins, of God as Maker and Keeper of the whole of our being, a fact to fill us richly with a sense of our lives and the world as gift. Such quiet reminds us that we are not responsible for our own flourishing. Our lives, our healing, our survival, our joy—all, all is gift.

This is the heart of what it means to keep the Sabbath, to take a day of rest, a concept I think we find increasingly difficult in the modern world. We are only a few generations removed from a time when commerce in many countries largely halted on Sundays in keeping with the strong biblical exhortations to "honor the Sabbath." In an internet age, when time is no longer marked by daylight or the limits of the embodied world, it is harder and harder to keep this command that also seems strange to our ears. Why shouldn't we work or buy? But in Scripture, the keeping of the Sabbath as a day of strict rest is not meant as a performance of righteousness but a return to faith, a homecoming to the benevolence in which the whole of our existence is rooted. By resting, we recollect that it is God who has made us and not we ourselves. All life and joy are the gift of his gracious hand.

God is the source of our halcyon days, and he is the surety for the healed world they allow us to glimpse. For the days of our rest set us in the larger light of God's goodness at work to remake all that is grieved and broken. As Abraham Joshua Heschel, the influential Jewish theologian, wrote, "Unless one learns how to relish the taste of Sabbath . . . one will be unable to enjoy the taste of eternity in the world to come."[4]

Those halcyon days . . . they lead us to heaven.

My faith has deeply shifted in the past ten years, perhaps particularly in the last few I've spent in trying to understand what it means to live a quiet life. In the beginning, I thought it would primarily mean I'd finally enact all the ideals I've held for so long: severe discipline with my phone and an ordered prayer life and silent evenings spent in contemplation rather than a television miniseries or distraction. I did not expect what I found. Whenever anyone asks me these days what my current book is about and I answer "Quiet," they usually laugh a little mockingly, eyeing my four small children or perhaps the church life my husband and I keep, along with its great reams of hospitable commitments. "I know," I respond, trying to accept the divine joke in good humor. "I've never had less quiet in my life. But I think, actually, that may be the point."

My search for quiet has unraveled my spiritual expectations. I am now more certain and less certain regarding my faith than I have ever been. What I am certain of is a grace that works in and alongside me so that my life equals more than it ought to. I cannot look at myself as I am without the weak-kneed knowledge that I have been helped. There is no other explanation for my survival or sanity, for the relationships that have weathered the great battering of my own and others' frailty, for the grief and loss my husband and I have suffered in the past years. In my life—not because it has lacked darkness and pain, frenzy or exhaustion, but precisely because it has run rife with those things—I can see that two plus two does not make four; it makes a peace much greater than I could have imagined.

I have watched so many people of faith deconstruct in the past difficult years, and I deeply understand the unraveling they feel. My own faith feels so different to me sometimes that it comes to my heart as a sort of unraveling. On a formal level, the level of my education with its long, expensive years spent delving into the doctrines of Christianity, I can honestly say that I am more than ever convinced of their veracity. What Christianity posits is ridiculous, but it is true. What makes the radical message of the gospel so wildly believable to me is how preposterous and gorgeous it is; the fact that God wants to *save* this world, save us, as we are—arrogant, fragile beings with wills blown wind wild, making havoc of creation yet also crafting a beauty that recalls our origin, embodying a preciousness that cannot be described without tears. That God counts these lives, this world, worthy of his own diminishment, and that he is, like me, a besotted mother capable of any sacrifice for my demanding, bumbling child, draws belief from me as the sight of a sleeping child draws my gasp of tenderness.

Where my own unraveling begins is with my sense of what is required to earn this gorgeous God's help. I am less certain, these days, of predicting how or when or in whom God might work because he seems to spring up, wild and merciful, in all the places I least expect him. I used to think him so demanding; I came to my quiet times as if God stood with arms crossed and back turned petulantly toward me until I said the right incantational prayer, confessed my small litany of sins, appeased his rightful grumpiness. I used to think he asked so much: holiness of life and a swift performance of righteous deeds and a clear conscience and constant prayer.

But in the turbulence of my last years, I have been able to offer him almost no fixity. I haven't sinned egregiously, and I've striven toward an inward attention to his words, but I haven't managed more than perfunctory and usually slightly desperate prayers aimed skyward in my brief moments of quiet in the morning. I have been exhausted for so long that I sometimes can't remember what it feels like to have something to offer my Creator in these snatched morning prayers. But he remains, and by his presence I am woven back together.

In that weaving, I understand the aching prayers that instigated this search for quiet have culminated not in my perfected striving but in rest. In a nourishment I did not earn. In halcyon quiet. In grace.

Sometimes I feel that I live in an old English novel.

Something by Trollope or Goudge, complete with the necessary church fetes and politics, tea and Victoria sponge, traditions that must not be changed, vestments in all the colors of the church year, with a redbrick vicarage behind the church and a wild garden presided over by a great willow woman of a tree. And the Eucharist.

I love my life as a vicar's wife and come easily to hospitality and gardening and the keeping of a big old home. It houses my soul quite nicely. But this life would be nothing but pretty trappings without the weekly feast that is the blood and cadence of its heart. The whole of it, with its old charms and small joys (and endless creaky frustrations too), draws life from the gift we celebrate each Sunday when we all troop into the echoey, freezing church and amble up to receive a little piece of bread in our hands, a sip of strong, ancient wine. A miniature feast in which the universe of our lives is rooted.

My spiritual journey in the past years has taken me many places. I deeply value the different branches of the church in which I've been raised and nourished. The rich scriptural heritage of my evangelical background with its potent call to a holy, missional life still drives my interaction with the world. I would not be without that rooting. But I have also come not just to love but to need the foundational support of liturgy and sacrament, of a form of worship that draws me into something that does not originate with my own effort or emotion. I treasure my involvement in a feast and gift, inaugurated at the Last Supper and completed on the cross, drawing me toward resurrection. Driven idealist that I am, it is far too easy for me to come to church as one more thing to do, to see worship as something I accomplish, an inward state dependent upon me. Rest rarely occurs to me in worship.

The Eucharist corrects me in that flawed way of thinking.

When I came to Oxford as a student and stumbled, my first week, through the doors of one of the "highest" churches in Oxford, with all the attendant smells and bells, I saw it as a space to explore. It fit my pageantry-loving, beauty-seeking soul. But what kept me coming (apart from the presence of the man who would become my husband) was the discipline I'd never encountered before, the weekly, if not daily, partaking in the Eucharist, receiving the bread and wine of communion as *the* root of my Christian life. Slowly, slowly, it transformed something in me, something that has always been a struggler. I wrestle mightily with God. I want more of him; I want more from myself. But as I came, with increasing frequency, to the feast of the Eucharist and realized the only task I had was to *receive*, it began to shift deep patterns in my soul.

Walking now for almost ten years in weekly (sometimes daily) company with the feast of the Eucharist has subtly changed the way I view my arrival at church. I come now to be fed. I come with open hands, aware of their emptiness as the very thing that qualifies my participation in the drama and gift of the feast.

Most weeks look the same for me right now. The children and I tromp in mere seconds before the first hymn opens the service. Since my husband is the priest, I am always in sole charge of our small folk, a task that means an almost ceaseless turn from one to the other throughout the hourlong service. There's precious little time for recollection or prayer. This used to worry me; I felt I came with nothing to offer, not even attention. Now, however harried I feel, when we all link hands and walk to the altar, I make sure my children are kneeling, and then, for an instant, I take that deep, deep breath that is the opening of all I am to the nourishment I need. In that quiet, I hold out my hand.

I have no doubt that I am fed.

In contemplating this, I've been struck lately by the way that Christ's gift of himself as bread in the Eucharist undoes the ancient curse of the fall. "By the sweat of your face, you will eat bread"[5] was Adam's punishment in the Genesis story of creation, though *consequence*, I think, would be the better word. Adam's choice to eat the fruit God asked him not to was a conscious decision to distrust the goodness and provision of God, to count it better to trust his own wit and muscle for blessing instead of his Maker. What else was going to happen but that he would eat his bread by the sweat of his brow? Not by gift or grace but by his own stubborn effort?

The Eucharist restores the bread of grace, the bread that is given, the life that flourishes because it is rooted in the generosity of God. No striving is needed here. No calculations of righteousness or effort. There is only this bread, given for us, by which we and the whole world will be healed. It's a halcyon quiet, there at the altar as I eat the bread, not of my striving but my rest.

That quiet branches into every moment of my week, each moment I step aside from the furor of the world into a space, however brief, of rest. The word *Eucharist* means "thanksgiving," and I am learning to see the quiet I enter as eucharistic in nature: both the place where God feeds me and the place where I receive with thanks. I am learning to enter each snatched moment of peace not with the expectation of effort but with the anticipation of gift. Here, strong arms will hold me. Here, I will be fed.

Here, I'll find that the only thing needed is to rest in the halcyon quiet of God.

Pray

O God, teach us that grace bears no calculation, that love will always exceed our effort. Help us to rest, that radical

*thing that cannot be measured but only received. Help us
to halt, to breathe, to abandon all need to perform our
prayer. Help us not to hold our own effort as mightier
than your grace but rather to sink, amazed and safe, into
love as it cradles our days. Through Jesus, who feeds us,
we pray, Amen.*

Ponder

- What is your first thought when you come to a time of
  dedicated quiet or prayer? Is there something you seek
  to give God in opening your time of devotion? What
  might it be, and do you think it helps or hinders your
  sense of his kindness?
- What place does rest take in your faith?
- When have you last known the grace of a truly restful
  day?

Part Three

The Gifts
of Quiet

9

Becoming Small

Assent and Amazement

A few months into my daughter's first year, there came a quiet moment. The late sun hung low in the sapphire sky I could see through my little Oxford rowhouse window. The light it shed was a gold rain that soaked the air and seeped in through the open window. I was stretched out on the couch, all jetlagged and sleepy, after a trip to America. Peonies sat on the table, just three in an old glass bottle, faces arcing toward the light.

Picture books lay piled on the floor, a trove of gems culled from my recent travels. A deep quiet fell around me that felt like gift and burden at the same time: no deadline or schedule, no place-to-be hurry reaching into that moment to drain its quiet, and yet there was a sense of restlessness at its back.

And my first child, Lilian: her baby weight rested full on my chest as I breathed on the couch in the gold-dust hush of a day that had been hot and now was healed by shadow. Her breath in its quick, infant rise and fall, the fragile rhythm I so often checked, afraid the music might cease. Her hands in their sleepy curl, their questing, tired grasp of my finger. Her head, nestled in under my chin, pushed up, up, up, always closer, as if she would shape my body to her curled little self once more.

And something, in that exact moment, yielded within me, not just to the thrust and nestle of that little head but to the larger demands that little body and being made upon the whole of my life. There is a crystalline clarity to my memory of that moment, as if it were outlined with a black pen, as I came to the understanding that, from her birth, I had withheld some sliver of myself from my daughter.

Such moments; we can never predict them. But when they find us, the world shifts within our hearts in such a way that everything looks different.

Before Lilian was born, I wrestled with pervasive anxiety. I kept asking my husband if something was wrong, and it stemmed from this unremitting back-of-my-psyche feeling that something was haywire, and I wouldn't be able to manage what was coming. I've learned that this fear is an integral aspect of pregnancy for me, another snaking branch of my mental illness, but I believe the phantoms my mind brings forth in early pregnancy are often a magnification of the spiritual fears already present in the secret places of my heart. I feared injury or catastrophe for us both. I feared death. I fretted about the challenge of raising a child in the modern world. I feared change—in my marriage, my time, my vision of the future. But the thing, I think in hindsight, I feared most?

Mundanity. Repetition. Countless days with no horizon beyond the care of a dependent child.

I wasn't afraid of the work; I was afraid of the meaninglessness. I'm most at home in books and big ideas. I love beauty and movement; I'm restless for adventure. The prospect of days mired in diapers, baths, and feeding, of mere sitting at home with a little person who wouldn't be able to carry on a conversation of any depth for years to come, left me profoundly anxious that I would wither in soul and personhood. Who would I become in a life made up not of great visions or books, not of academic connections or publishing accomplishments or literary creation or notoriety, but of the mire of very little things?

I had so feared the loss of my essential being to the service of this scrap of personhood that I thought I needed to keep some reserve, some sense of my independence, of the life I might live apart from her, in spite of her. I wept the night she was born when I realized I would never be autonomous again; some part of me would always walk abroad in the world, someone who was also not me, and that required a total relinquishment of myself I was not sure I could give.

But that day, in the late afternoon light, with its strange alchemy of exhaustion and affection and bright, burnished quiet, I understood that the love into which I had entered with my child required the whole of myself, not even a morsel held back. I stood in the presence of something I did not fully understand; I could not glimpse what I might become if I opened the hands of my inmost self and let that last sliver of selfhood join the ocean of my love. But what I knew in that moment was that the terms of this love were of total assent, of utter gift.

And in the great quiet, I gave it.

"He who is faithful in a very little thing is faithful also in much."[1]

133

Jesus said this as part of a parable exploring trustworthiness, but I hear the words in my mom's voice, one of the phrases she used continuously on my siblings and me when we were teens and most small disciplines seemed beyond us. It's a radical phrase, that. I didn't hear the subversiveness of it as an annoyed teen, but now, when I think of what it implies, when I survey the smallness of my own life in service of my children, I am astonished.

We aren't really taught to value little things in our world or to be faithful in them. From the close of our childhood, we're taught to reach for the stars, to trust and value those who accomplish big things. As if the bigness of an accomplishment, an audience, a sales figure, a degree, an idea proves their worth. Trust what is big, follow what is mighty and successful, give everything to become this too. I must confess I hesitated to open this chapter with a story about motherhood because so often the insight culled from the care of children is seen, even by those who think they value it, as too small for universal application or spiritual insight.

But Jesus claimed, and lived, the opposite.

I mean, obviously, he said the kingdom of heaven was made up of those who had hearts like children. But he also and almost continuously refused the importance, the bigness and visibility, that we seem to think is so vital for influence or significance in the modern world.

I've been reading the Gospel of John each morning before sitting down to write this book, and I've been amused and a little disturbed in myself by how often Jesus confounded his disciples and all the people who loved him by his refusal to walk the paths of influence or visibility that everyone thought he should. They kept on thinking he would, in some way, storm the gates of power. They kept waiting for him to declare his authority and worth in such a way that he could rally a right army to his aid. And he . . . healed grungy, desperate people and told them to keep it a secret. He spoke in parables that children might love but adults misunderstand, ducked out of sight, and went up on lonely mountains by himself. He cuddled children and went to houses of ill repute and pursued power-less people.

One particular cycle of this theme within John's story has struck me deeply in these past months of writing. It opens with Jesus's feeding of the five thousand in chapter 6. A triumphal murmur thrummed through the latter part of the story, as the well-fed crowd suddenly found themselves capable of total faith in enigmatic Jesus, because the literal feeding of thousands . . . that's the sort of thing great rulers did. That's regime-change stuff—proof you can muster enough resources to crush those who might challenge your authority. The crowd wanted to crown him king right there on the spot—king of their spot of earth, a king in place of the Roman rulers yet one with a Roman sort of power. I think the disciples must have stood by, watching, thinking *This is the moment when our choice for this man will be proved right.*

And Jesus . . . hid. He withdrew to the mountains. They couldn't find him, and thus they couldn't king him or force upon him a power he did not seek or approve.

Thus follows a series of little dramas that leave those who follow Jesus utterly confounded in their notions of influence and power and belief. First, Jesus walked across the windy lake in the dark of the night, overtaking the terrified disciples in their boat, men who must have thought their erstwhile king had abandoned them because he would not fulfill the role they

135

thought he should bear. The well-fed crowd (perhaps now a little hungry again) caught up with him in the daylight on the other side the next morning, but before they could get well started, Jesus called their bluff. They followed him because he fed them a bit of bread, and they wanted that physical feeding guaranteed—not because it was a sacrament, not because they glimpsed the divine generosity, the mercy and grace, made tangible in that feast. Don't work for a few bites of fish and bread, he said. Do the works of God in order to earn the sort of food that gives you eternal life.

They were hooked. What kind of food was this? They were still thinking in terms of enchanted crumbs, talismans, power bound up by a secret knowledge that would be given to them if they "[worked] the works of God," as enigmatic Jesus puts it in verse 28. They're thinking riches and Rome overthrown. Fine, they asked. What are these works? We're ready.

And Jesus's answer: Believe in me.

Mere belief. Trust in God's generosity and mercy. That is the "secret" work of those who would be transformed by bread from heaven. And what is that bread from heaven? Just Jesus, come to die. No power to be grabbed. No Gnostic secret knowledge. No spell. Just . . . belief in a God who would give his own Son as bread to feed a world marked not just by hunger of the belly but hunger of the heart and mind and soul, a hunger as large as eternity that only God could fill.

A little later in John, when the crowds caught up with Jesus again, he said much the same thing but with a further challenge: "If anyone is willing to do His will, he will know of the teaching, whether it is of God or whether I speak from Myself."[2]

We don't even get to start with a full explanation in place, we don't even get that much of the kingdom steady in our hands. Partly because we don't even yet know what we ought to desire. We can only know, can only gain God's kingdom, from the inside of obedience. We can only progress in this upside-down realm by the smallest of decisions in the secret place of our hearts, and the smallest of choices that enact it thoroughly. Do what I say; believe.

Compared to the defeat of armies and the toppling of Roman emperors, to the feeding of thousands and the ruling of thrones, the sheer act of belief in Christ seems the tiniest thing possible.

And so, so many find themselves incapable of this tiny act.

What is small?
Children are small.
Seeds are small.
Moments are small.
Yet of these the whole world is composed.

What was it I feared I would lose in yielding my life to the littleness of my daughter's needs? I think I feared much the same things as those crowds following Jesus. They knew the potency of Roman power, the pragmatic quality of demonstrable authority. The power of trust, of love, what is that in the face of tyrants? I was tortured with similar doubt in early motherhood. If I gave up my scratched little handhold on power, my sliver of influence, my tiny chunk of online presence, my studies, my capacity even to define myself by what I produced, then who would I be?

There's no success in being defined by the amount of yourself that you give away.

Unless you are a seed, yielding yourself to the loamy earth of a love you don't fully understand, letting it tear you open so that a new person, a new way of being, may emerge.

Unless you are God, giving the whole of divinity away in order to be buried, a cluster of cells, in the dark earth of a woman's womb.

Unless you are Mary, accepting God into your womb, entering a story that might tear open your heart in its beauty but one you know is worth the gift of all that you have.

Much has been written about Mary's fiat (Latin for the phrase "let it be done"), her assent to the story God told about her that she was invited into by the yielding of herself. *Assent* is an odd word, not often used. We're all familiar with *consent*, the idea of giving permission to another for "something to happen" (as Dictionary.com says). Consent bears a certain specificity and, with it, a certain control: I can withhold my consent, and this thing shall not happen. But *assent* bears a different idea of power. To assent, as almost all the dictionaries agree, is to agree with or approve something that is already present. My assent will not change the circumstances; it will only change me. It is my orientation to or cooperation with a circumstance already present as fact.

Assent at its best bears the idea of willingness as gift. It's something that can only be given. You don't have to assent or agree with what is before you, and often you ought not to; but if you do, it is something offered, a yielding to a story you perhaps didn't choose and don't yet fully understand. Poet Denise Levertov wrote of Mary that "Courage unparalleled / opened her utterly," and this is what I find myself called to enter in the quiet moments of my love.[3]

The invitation to assent is one of the great but often unmarked gifts of quiet.

Levertov also wrote in her poem about Mary that for all of us, there are "moments / when roads of light and storm / open from darkness in a man or woman."[4] The choice comes to us as well: we, too, are invited into the great quiet of assent to God's story as it unfolds within our lives, an assent that is not won from us by coercion or guilt but one we enter by the offering of our faith. And so often the assent we give is not to an epic deed or heroic single task but to the contours of our lives as they are, in their littleness. Assent to the faithfulness in small things is the condition, in Jesus's opinion, of knowing the reality of God.

I assent to finding God in the very places I least expected him, no longer demanding he show up in my life as lightning and thunder to remove me from all my little obligations and make me great. Rather I find him in the pith of those tiny things, at the heart of my need and the needs of all those I serve.

I have come to believe that the gift and work of quiet is not to be found in the reaching of great feats but the keeping of small faithfulnesses. The work of quiet is never about becoming more powerful by our accumulation of its presence. Rather, moment by moment, we detach ourselves from a way of thinking that sees worth only in size and force, that sees significance only in self-assertion. From the roil of loud, competing voices we step aside to listen, to let the larger beauty of God's own littleness, his own assent, dwell within the inmost spaces of our hearts. In this choice we daily become those who, in the words of an Old Testament prophet, know not to "[despise] the day of small things."[5]

Thing is, the world in its mystery is made up of little things. And in holy assent, we receive it all back again as miracle.

———

One of my favorite novels is *Lila* by Marilynne Robinson. Many people are now familiar with her first novel, *Gilead*, composed of letters written by an old pastor to the young son who is the startlement and miracle and ache of his old age. *Lila* is the story of that son's mother, a drifter who wandered into the town of the old preacher with questions that stirred his heart and soul. They marry, but it takes her a long time to reconcile her life as a forgotten and neglected child, her loneliness and wandering, her shadowed past, with the faith that drew her to her husband. We see the world through Lila's eyes, but early on we realize she has been so shaped by rejection and loss that she cannot view anything or anyone with trust. Her marriage, in its beginning, she views almost as a moment of weakness, when her need for shelter and affection rendered her defenseless.

But the novel is a story of healed vision, of a soul transformed by the possibility of a love that will not leave or fail, by the rumor of a grace that may just wash over all the evil she has known. The story is of Lila's slow assent to a generosity and grace she cannot fully comprehend, a care for her in her insignificance she cannot understand but only assent to receive. Her assent comes day by day, inch by inch, in the tiny moments of which a whole life is composed. There's one scene late in the novel, when Lila stands pregnant in the kitchen and begins to imagine what it might mean to trust, to love, to stay, and she tells the baby in her belly,

> If we stay here, soon enough it will be you sitting at the table and me, I don't know, cooking something, and the snow flying, and the old man so glad we're here he'll be off in his study praying about it. And geraniums in the window. Red ones.[6]

In that moment of imagining the most ordinary of days with the smallest of beauties—red geraniums—Lila assents to a story defined by trust and love. This is expressed in her renewed capacity to engage the tiniest moments of the ordinary as portents of miracle and love. When the reader finds Lila thinking in this way one knows, one *knows*, that she has crossed some great Rubicon. She's seeing through the eyes of love; she has finally accepted love as the vision by which she will behold her life, and in that assent the world begins to glimmer, to gleam, to unfold itself to her imagination in a workaday miracle that is sweeter than anything she has known.

We're like Lila. In the kind of assent we give to God's story, we are always given back a transformed vision. We move from the wastescape of a world defined by competition and anxiety to one illumined by amazement. In our assent to the intimacy and littleness of our daily faith, we find ourselves walking amidst a mercy we could not earn, could not conjure, will never deserve. We enter its infinitude moment by miraculous little moment, as the world unfolds once more to us in its particularity, its intimacy, its beauty.

I read about Lila and her geraniums again during one of the longer pandemic lockdowns here in England, when I felt nearly maddened by confinement with small children, by isolation, by the enclosure of our home. I read that passage one afternoon and walked a little desolately into my cold kitchen to start dinner for that evening. On the long windowsill over the sink sat a little earthen pot of miniature daffodils, just opened in the late, wintered sunlight. Each green, pointed leaf was like a reaching hand, each fragile flower a face hungering for the light that was its life. They were tiny and frail and, to me, in that moment, the total sign and sacrament of the grace still invading the enclosure of our lives in that dark season.

I sat down just to look at them and understood, like Lila in her moment of imagination, either everything matters or it doesn't. Either those tiny things on the window are a portent revealing the care God gives to all little things—to flowers in the field and finches in the blackened winter branches and little, grumpy children and weary, lonelyhearted women who find it hard not to feel forgotten—or they aren't.

With all my heart, I believe they are.

And this is the knowledge to which we are daily, achingly summoned by the quiet that waits for our assent and the grace that waits to amaze us by transforming our little moments of waking and sleeping, fresh baked bread and children's feet, morning air and red geraniums . . . into the stuff of lifelong joy.

Pray

O God, who formed this world as gift and crafted us out of your own overflowing joy, help us to open hand and heart to all that you offer. Give us grace to agree with the story you are weaving amidst the little things of our lives. Teach us assent—the gift of our own selves in response to yours. Teach us amazement, as the world returns to us reclothed in wonder. Let us laugh like children and sing with the awe of angels as we watch your story unfold amidst our ordinary hours. Through the love of your Son, Jesus, healer of our sight and lightener of our eyes, Amen.

Ponder

- Take a moment to be still and look around you; let the fullness of the present enter your senses. What goodness do you find?

- Consider the different realms of your life; which have you dismissed as too small for amazement or meaning? Ask God to kindle that specific place with wonder once more.

- What does assent mean to you? Is it something you can offer to the larger story of your life? Why or why not?

10

Wise Woman's Cottage

Imagination

The spot was carefully chosen, the day cool, the autumn wind companionable.

I liked the spice of cold and the must of dead leaves that scented the air. I sat with my back nestled against the trunk of a spindly old oak. Our yard wasn't large, but even at age eight my choice for hush was instinctual, and I'd managed to nestle in a spot where my siblings wouldn't quickly find me, tucked in the trees that clustered round the back fence and trying for a glimpse of the wild beyond. Quiet settled around me, soaked through me like water, and I let myself breathe . . . and listen. I had come to the crafting of my first poem, and already I knew keenly that what I needed was not just to think but attend; in writing my poem I was as much a witness as a wordsmith.

I had a lined notebook in hand, the sort in which small people practice handwriting, and I labored fixedly over my scratched words. Looking back now, I understand that what I wanted to describe was the pageantry of creation, its interconnectedness, its internal meaning, this sense that all the various wonders I encountered in my outdoor prowls were parts of a symphony or a story, something that *meant* in a potent way.

The glimpses I found of stars and sunlight through the window in my cubbyhole of a bedroom were an astonishment to me. I was thrilled by caterpillars in their scrunch and mystery. I tracked butterflies in a kind of awe and traced the inscrutable paths of beetles. Every day I woke to a different set of birds lacing their song through the branches outside my window. I had a chart by which I identified the new ones when they landed, their names whispered and savored on my tongue evoking far lands and exotic stories: *titmouse, tanager, black-capped chickadee*. Even as I stalked all these small, daily wonders, climbing trees and crawling through the grass, there was a part of my inmost self that stood aside, hushed and watchful, understanding that all this meant something more than itself, something generous and good. By making a poem, I wanted to respond to it, reach through it to grasp the presence at its heart.

So it's the strain I most remember about my composition, the sense of almost frustrated yearning I bore to give language to the way the world was a story telling itself to me in each disclosive, daily form. I wanted to describe and join the goodness it revealed, a narrative of ceaseless creation and re-creation, of splendor and terror and birth. My words even then seemed spare and frail to me. Now I smile at their neat, rhymed piety; I'd drawn from a limited inner ragbag of vocabulary and religious language to express my deepest thoughts.

But I'm also astonished at that child, my early self, because however incapable I felt of describing it, eight-year-old me had already encountered and engaged the holy, formative power of imagination. I understood in those early days that there were different ways to know the world. I was a good little scientist; I made a museum of natural history in my room, lining two shelves with the feathers and stones and cocoons I collected every day. I labeled them, learned their names from the Audubon guides on our family bookshelves. That was one way of knowing, but I also knew that poetry was another. Story too. Song. And it was to those I turned in my quest for both knowledge and expression when my own sense of amazement and desire grew too heavy and sweet to keep inside my small body.

Quiet led me to a space of creation.

It's easy to look back on childhood or even an earlier season of adult life with the diamond lens of nostalgia. I'm sure there was just as much fallenness and struggle around me as there is now, but there was also a lot more boredom. That's putting it in negative terms, because I know it now for one of the great gifts of my formation. The hours of late afternoon stretched empty each day; I could play outdoors, I could read a book, I could craft or draw or find a few friends and siblings to entertain me. But often those hours opened and closed in a great swathe of independent solitude. In that space, so difficult to cull these days for child and adult alike, I gained one of the great gifts of quiet: imagination.

To know the world in such a way that one can touch the surface but also reach through the outer facets to the love that pulses in all beautiful things, to be gripped in turn by the goodness beyond them; such knowing is *imagination*. And in the long silences I found out of doors, in the wide space I had to inwardly question, to ponder, to scratch out my poems or make up my stories, I learned what it meant for imagination to be one of the great languages of truth.

Such knowing is natural to every human born, our heritage via our creation as beings in God's image, the one whose own divine imagination formed the world through which we move in such yearning curiosity. But to enter the fullness of this gift requires a mind capable of wonder. It needs the watchful space of a listening, seeking quiet in which we may move beyond the surfaces we see into the inmost realms of ourselves. Imagination asks of us a quiet space where we may attend to all that sings to us from outside the walls of time, from the deathless world in which our hearts seek roots.

What *is* imagination, and what bearing does it have upon our search for quiet?

I think we must answer with story first. In George MacDonald's fairy tales, there's a fascinating theme that often occurs: the wise woman's cottage. Those who enter it think they are walking into a humble little house, usually with just one room, perhaps in a forest or perched by the side of the sea. But once inside, they discover a door in each wall. To walk through even one is the opening of a great adventure. Vast halls and other worlds, the past and the future, forests and caves—each door from that cottage might lead to anywhere else in the world . . . or out of it. The cottage is bigger on the inside than the outside, a space of seemingly unfettered discovery from which and through which all manner of great quests might lead.

I think we each have a wise woman's cottage in our minds, and that is the inward space of our imagination. We bear interior worlds; do you know this? Can you remember the moments of childhood in which you looked out some window in your soul upon a place or story, an image or word that stirred you with yearning hope? That inward house; we each have it, that cottage of the mind in which we will always find endless doors leading out from ourselves into story and song, vision and prayer.

The psalms speak over and over about the inward place of the heart, what my trusty old *Strong's Concordance* describes as the "inner man, mind, will, heart, soul, understanding," the seat of appetite and emotion, passion and courage.[1] This is the place Jesus means when he says it is the things that come forth from our hearts that defile us. It's also the place indicated when he says, "Blessed are the pure in heart, for they shall see God."[2] I believe imagination is integral to what Scripture means when it speaks of the inward person, the realm of the heart. Imagination is the way we translate the world to ourselves, the inner room in which our outward vision is interpreted by our "in" sight. We all deal in imagination each day of our lives.

We cannot escape some sense that we are enmeshed in a larger story in which we are agents for good or ill.

We cannot create what we have not imagined.

We cannot love without an inward idea of the person we hold so precious.

We cannot grow without entering that inmost room, opening the doors that lead us deeper into vivid images of all we might make or become.

But many of us have lost the way to that house, have forgotten that this inward place of potent meaning is our native land. We talk much in the modern world of introverts and extroverts, of those who like to be alone and those who really can't stand it, those more creative and those more driven to action. And we run as much as we talk—from this post to that screen, from this meeting to that call—never halting long enough to even remember the aching rooms within our hearts. We speak of these proclivities as if they are optional ways of being guided by preference, as if our need for hush, our need to excavate and understand the inmost rooms of ourselves and all that open from them isn't fundamental to each human being alive.

What *is* imagination?

The inmost room from which we glimpse God at play in the world and among the people he has so lovingly made.

The wise woman's cottage with its doors leading to the story we might live, the art we might make, the song we might sing, the hero we might become, the prayer we might offer; our window upon the eternal.

And the way to that room? It's straight and sure. We just follow the paths of quiet that lead to the holy, enchanted door.

There once was a boy named Jack who knew the potent beauty of imagination. It was mighty in him, the consolation and companion of a boyhood that saw the death of his mother and months spent away from home in difficult boarding schools. When he was little, he glimpsed something ancient and perfect in a tiny toy garden, a perfect refuge, an Eden lost. Little though he was, the sight of that garden struck an ache in him as big as the world. When he grew older, the beauty came in the words of an old Norse poem about a young, beloved god whose death struck an anguished lament: "Balder the beautiful / is dead, is dead."[3] And in those words, the boy Jack felt his heart rise up, felt the inmost rooms of his mind stirred by the wind from an open window within his imagination, one that looked out upon a world in which a god could die for love and beauty could last beyond the touch of sorrow. Those moments—he named them

"Joy"—were the best things Jack knew, the secret treasure he bore into the opening years of his manhood.

The problem for Jack was that, like many of us, he didn't believe that any of what he so treasured within himself was true.

Jack was a child of the modern age, schooled in science experiments and logical proofs. He didn't really believe in a realm of the heart or the truth of great stories, much less that those things might lead him to enter the room of his own imagination to discover that the beauty he loved came from a Person calling to him from the other side. It took years of reading, years of wrestling, and a great friend (who was also a brilliant writer) writing a poem[4] about artistry and imagination as things we bear because we were made in the image of an imaginative God before Jack came to grasp that all the beauty he loved might just be true.

That boy grew up to be C. S. Lewis, a mighty advocate not just of the Christian faith but of imagination as fundamental to the way we come to know what is true about God, ourselves, and the world. Embracing the truth of imagination, its potent reality, was crucial to his conversion.

Jack recognized that one of the major obstacles to knowing God in the modern world was the idea that we can only discover what is true by logic. Even those who live by faith in "things not seen"[5] still struggle to understand what that means and the grace that comes from imagining a world we haven't yet encountered. As Lewis worked to articulate this, he wrote a fascinating little essay called "Meditation in a Toolshed."[6] In it, he asks his readers to picture a man standing in a darkened garden toolshed, watching a beam of light come over the door. From inside that shed, there are two different ways the man could "see" the world outside, and thinking about them could help us understand the different ways all of us discover truth, especially through imagination.

The first view of the world came to the man in Lewis's essay by looking right at the beam. Lewis describes this as "contemplation," the kind of knowledge we get by looking "at" a thing or experience, something we can only have by standing apart from it. This is the knowing of scientists and mathematicians, expressed in a language of logic and reason. This is one way to know what is true.

But the opposite view comes when the man in the essay steps into the sunbeam, entering the light, not only experiencing the warm glow of the light itself but looking along it into the green and summer world outside. This, Lewis calls "enjoyment," the kind of truth that comes to us from inside an experience. We know love not by observing it in someone else but by literally being within it ourselves. We find ourselves capable of courage when we imagine the story we might enact or the hero we might become, or when music stirs us in a language without words. Such knowing comes in the language of image and song, story and poem, an equal source of truth to the language of logic.

I found Lewis's essay in a season when I was struggling to articulate why my experiences of beauty were so vital to my faith. At that time, my imagination was still rich and mighty, and my problem was not so much that I could not dwell within it as that I had learned to distrust what it told me. I, too, was a child of the modern world, and the older I got, the more I found myself immersed in the kind of thinking that set "truth" only within the confines of reason, argument, observation, and proof. Most of what kept me alive in those years was beyond definition: affection, music, fantastical stories, and mountain walks that somehow healed my heart. Reading Lewis's story allowed me to reclaim the awed joy I knew as a child when I wrote that first poem, to trust what I found as I ventured through the great doors of beauty and story.

I still revel in that knowledge.

And yet I've come to understand I'm still in grave danger of diminishing the holy power of imagination.

As I have wrestled with the subject of quiet, as I have returned to a study of imagination, I have realized that my capacity to imagine, to experience God's reality in a direct and joyous way, is threatened almost constantly not by the forces of science but by those of technology. I see everything through a screen. I didn't really notice the way this was happening at first; I joined Instagram like everyone else and took pleasure in composing a photo journal of my life. When my children were born, it seemed the most natural thing in the world to walk around with phone in hand to catch those moments of almost unbearable sweetness.

But when I returned recently to Lewis's essay, I realized that the function of a phone is always to set one outside of an experience. If Joy is something we know from the inside of laughter and affection, if it is something we can only know in a taste-and-see way, an immersive encounter, then the act of stepping outside those experiences in order to record them is a move from Enjoyment to Contemplation. When I mediate the whole of my experience through my camera, whipping it out at every hint of intense or immersive experience, I'm ending the very thing I set out to record. I am jolted back to a place where I'm standing apart from the thing I want to capture. I'm no longer *in* the grace of the beauty I have recorded.

Something that troubles me deeply is a nagging sense that imagination may be in danger these days, not from an over-emphasis on reason but from our trained incapacity to simply receive the world without recording it. If our most sublime experiences turn us not inward, to that room with windows looking out on eternity, but outward, to a screen where we can edit, trim, and share with the world, then I fear we will become incapable of receiving what sublimity arrives to communicate in the first place.

What kind of a life is that?

What kind of a story does that offer to all of us still mired in a broken world? What escape is offered if sublimity and beauty themselves lead us not to God but to the echo chamber of our own and everyone else's critique? How will we engage with a story beyond the confines of our own brokenness or a beauty beyond the touch of our despair?

In the past years, a great deal of research has emerged outlining the negative effects of smartphone use on teenagers. The research is dire and clear; such usage increases depression, anxiety, and self-harm. Much has been said in response about the way our technologies magnify peer pressure, bombard young minds with images of impossible perfection, and leave them open to critique and attack by vicious people. Our imaginations are formed by what we feed them, and if the scream of the online world is what we feed ourselves and our children, then our inner rooms will become echo chambers for all the voices that threaten to destroy us.

But perhaps even worse, I wonder if we will be left incapable of joy—of Lewis's Joy and my childhood knowings, those moments of amazement in which a world beyond our broken one looms close. If the attention of eye and heart are addictively mired in a screen that is a sleepless tool of analyzation, critique, and distraction, then there is no room for imagination. No time for the stories that might let us remember ourselves as agents in God's great tale. There is no chance for beauty to catch us unawares and jolt us awake to all that can be hoped, for Joy to stab us alive to the goodness that might lurk with healing in its wings—lurk just beyond the furor of the online world (which is just the same old devilish world it has always been, now available 24/7 to our compulsive, desperate eyes).

To step back from the madness, setting down the phone and sinking into the quiet might be our first step, and the first step of the young souls we love, into a realm where hope and joy and innocence are even possible, where courage and kindness are even *imaginable* once more.

From the time my children were tiny, I've read them fantastical stories. Well, all sorts of stories, really, but we seem to have a particular penchant for stories where knights and fair maidens tilt swords with dragons, where fair and foul are locked in battle, and good-hearted souls save the day. Such tales, I think, speak to the inmost places of my children's hearts, where mystery broods and other worlds await their discovery. But one of my children is of a pragmatic turn of mind, and ever since they could speak has often asked me, when we read such tales, "Is that princess actually in our world? Is that dragon real?"

I always pause before I answer. I understand that the questions are of a practical and not philosophical nature, so I usually answer with the straight-up honesty demanded by small children: No, but there are things like dragons in our world. There are people as beautiful in soul or spirit as that princess.

But lately my small boy, Samuel, has become captivated by the tale of St. George and his slaying of the dragon. I don't show my children many "scary" books, but I grew up with this one and thought I'd try it on them one day. I mostly expected to close the book and try again in a couple of years. But Samuel was fixated in a wondrous way. I was a little astonished. He's three, my boy, and the one (gorgeous) book we have recounting this legend is written in high style and meant for much older readers.[7] Not to mention the dragon in the illustrations is a terror. The wounds depicted on both knight and beast make me squirm, and the savagery of the dragon's face is viscerally real. But so is the beauty. St. George is kind and brave, the great figure on every page, with a holy anguish in his face, grit in his hands, and a gentle love for Una, the princess who sought a hero to save her kingdom from destruction.

Samuel asks for this book to be read aloud again and again. He has begun to raid the dress-up chest for costumes to make himself "the Red Cross Knight." He has one red shirt in constant rotation because when he wears it, he's closest in color to his hero. The story has entered the inmost room of his heart and is shaping the way he sees the world. I've found him poring over it quietly on the couch and have watched him, realizing the way this tale is shaping his imagination.

When we came, this year, to the keeping of Michaelmas, the feast of St. Michael the Archangel, great slayer of the dragon Satan (a much more prominent festival in England than in the States), I pulled out Samuel's favorite book again as part of our reading and discussion. I told the children the story of Michael, the great warrior angel sent by God to war against Satan and all the hosts of evil. I told them they, too, were meant to be brave, to resist what was wicked and fight well for God.

"Like St. George, Mama," said Samuel. "I can be brave like him. Mama, are dragons real?"

As always, I paused. But this time, as I swiftly pondered my answer, I thought of a G. K. Chesterton quote I've always loved:

> Fairy tales do not give the child his first idea of bogey. What fairy tales give the child is his first clear idea of the possible defeat of bogey. The baby has known the dragon intimately ever since he had an imagination. What the fairy tale provides for him is a St. George to kill the dragon.[8]

I realized, abruptly, that in his engagement with the mighty story of St. George, Samuel was entering a place in imagination where he could conceive of that courage as something he might enact himself.

So, "Yes," I said. "They are. You can't always see them like in the story, but dragons are real, and God will make you strong to fight them."

He nodded in great determination, and I have no doubt that when he is confronted with evil, the world he has found in *Saint George and the Dragon* will come to his aid.

Yes, Samuel, dragons are real. So are angels and demons. So are high priests over heaven and mighty kings and great queens and a Savior with a face like fire and a heart as gentle as a lamb's. So much is real that is beyond our sight. The things of the earth that we understand as absolute are rooted in a reality much greater, subtler, and lovelier than we have ever experienced. But sometimes we can imagine it. When we step aside into the spacious halls of hush, when we enter a story or sojourn with a song, when we look into the heart of the beauty and drama cramming the world at our fingers, we enter that inmost room from which many doors lead onward to a world we have only begun to desire.

Prayer

O God, *who speaks in story, sings in starlight, and crafts an inmost world within our hearts, teach us to look beyond the surface of the outer world as through a window, beholding the wondrous light that falls upon us from the realms of heaven. Help us to nourish our inmost selves, to keep airy and clean that room where our dreams dwell and our hope waits and the doors to all creation are in our grasp. Help us to trust the great stories, to live the great songs, to fight the dragons and keep the feasts, through Christ, the Great Knight of heaven and of our yearning hearts, Amen.*

Ponder

- Do you think all people are imaginative? Why or why not? What form does your imagination take?
- What stories have helped you to understand the story of your own life?
- What doors open from the wise woman's cottage in your heart?

11

Seeing from the Inside

Conviction and Courage

If I could get away with naming one of my children Aragorn, I would.

I refrain due to the fear they might be haunted by the aura of intense Tolkien nerdiness such a name might entail. I want my children to consider their names a gift, not a millstone round the neck (though this hasn't stopped me from giving each a name with a fantastical literary connotation). But naming always confers a kind of story. Names come with histories, and if there's one story I wish I could bequeath as a kind of prophecy or companion to one of my children, it might just be the tale of Aragorn/Strider, the king who waited and suffered, who served and returned.

Not, though, for the warrior's might and trekker's prowess he embodies through much of the action in *The Lord of the Rings*. The Aragorn I so admire is the one we hear about as a rumor before the story gets going, whose history fills the appendices, who walked the wilderness for decades *before* the adventure began. He was Strider then, treading lonely roads and serving the small, a king by rights who lived as a servant wanderer. The conquering Aragorn, the skilled warrior and wise king we meet in the climax of Tolkien's epic, would not have been possible if he had not first been the grey-cloaked wanderer who humbled himself to aid a bunch of recalcitrant hobbits, who carried the ancient stories in his heart, and who listened to the wisdom of his elders.

It took me a couple of reads before I realized how necessary the wintered years of Aragorn's life were to the summertime of his action. I read Tolkien's opus in my seventeenth year, and I've made no secret of the way it saved my faith. Newly diagnosed with mental illness, appalled that God would allow such a thing to come upon me, I'd abandoned the reading of Scripture and could barely look the thought of faith in the face. In his mercy and humor, God set a fantastical epic in my hands instead. There, I discovered a way to navigate darkness, to choose courage, to recognize the dignity of indomitable hope. The first time I read it, what drew my eyes were the dramatic choices, the anguished reach for courage, the defiant defense of beauty.

The second time I read it, I'd entered a new season: the fallow years of learning to cope with a broken mind that would never go away. The drama had faded and now there was just a great deal of difficult quiet. Aragorn taught me what to do with that silence, how to walk the grey days of my sojourn. For though born to the kingship of the race of men in Middle Earth, he lived for decades in exile with little might at his disposal. His power lay almost entirely in his choice of whom to heed, whose voice he would allow to shape the years of his waiting.

Tolkien makes it clear that Aragorn was a listener.

He spoke little and heeded "the wise" (a theme that runs like quicksilver through the story). Early in his life, Aragorn chose Elrond as his mentor, trusting this wise and patient Elf-lord who understood the story and place to which Aragorn had been born, who taught him to treasure his heritage but also to wait for his kingship until the time was ripe and his character formed. Aragorn also chose to heed Gandalf the wizard, a sort of pilgrim angel sent by the powers over the sea (Tolkien's "divine" figures) to kindle courage and hope in those who were called to resist evil. Aragorn listened to all the wisdom of Gandalf's humility, his patience. He waited and hoped. Had he not spent those years in that faithful, patient listening, he might easily have sought his throne too soon, asserted a power he did not have, become a tyrant conqueror instead of the tempered, gracious king "whose hands were those of a healer."[1]

With Aragorn in mind, I began to spot the themes of listening at work in each of Tolkien's characters; every hero and villain in the tale is profoundly formed by the voices they allow to shape their inmost thoughts. The villain wizard Saruman, once good and wise, is shaped by the cunning narration of Sauron to believe that coercive power is the only way to rule. Denethor, once a wise steward of a great people, is equally swayed by Sauron's voice, made incapable of anything but despair. Even Éowyn, noble sword maiden of Rohan, is for a time convinced that death is the only freedom because she heeds the whispers of a traitor.

The heroes are equally formed by their listening.

Frodo listens to Gandalf and makes the courageous choice to offer himself as the quiet hero for his time by taking the evil ring to destruction. Faramir, wise and gentle where his brother, Boromir, is selfish and brash, is known as the "wizard's boy" because he seeks the ancient tales and heeds the voice of

Gandalf. Samwise, too, the simple gardener hobbit, attends to Gandalf's tales and understands himself as taking part in a great story through his faithful service to Frodo.

When I discovered all of this in the long quiet of my own desolate season, I began to understand very clearly that the voices we allow to speak in the innermost rooms of our hearts are the ones that will tell our stories. My own choice in that season would shape my next ten years. I realized I could listen to the voice of my mental illness, to the narrative of pain and suffering that dragged me toward a sense of random, rank despair. Or I could attend to the story told by beauty, in the arc of Aragorn's narrative, in the love of my parents—even once again in the great narrative of Scripture, that difficult, wild tale of our brokenness and our healing where one particular Voice could sing me forward into hope.

I chose the latter. And in the great hush of that season, I began to listen with a fixity and attention that rooted the whole of my faith.

Our identity is driven by our listening.

Our faith is formed by the voices we choose to heed; our convictions are built upon the stories they tell us about ourselves and the world. But we cannot listen without quiet. We cannot untangle the great chorus of voices driving our sense of self unless we step into a space of chosen hush. Sometimes the quiet seems fallow, like Aragorn's grey years, like my barren decade of illness. But the spacious silence of such seasons often allows us to push aside the many fears we've half believed, the wrong things we've embraced, the voices whose stories prod us toward greater brokenness rather than toward health. Quiet allows us a holy autonomy in which we are given ownership of our inmost world once more, the chance to discern and empower which voices will form our choices.

"My sheep hear My voice and . . . follow Me"[2] says Jesus, and I've always been intrigued by this assertion, this proclamation that a right and holy listening is integral to our belief. That faith rests not primarily on gritted will or savvy choice but on response, on a honed and holy capacity to hear. I think that idea echoes through Scripture. How many of the Bible's great heroes were drawn into the wilderness so they could encounter their God? How did God describe himself, his own voice to Elijah, but as the "gentle blowing," or as the old King James Version has it, a "still small voice" that endures when all the cacophony of the world has died away?[3]

My sheep hear my voice, and I know them . . .

We can attend to God's voice in full trust precisely because we are already known and beloved to the one who calls. I find it marvelous to know that, in faith, I'm singled out by the voice of God. This is one of the great graces of quiet. When I listen for God's voice, I find he doesn't just speak generally; he speaks particularly, to me. Quiet restores us to the wondrous autonomy of finding that God truly does come to speak to those who love him as Father and Friend. Of course we listen, and that kind of listening can change the course of our lives in ways it's hard to imagine until they're whispered to us by the God who called a world into being out of the shadows.

But ah, it's hard to do.

There are so very many voices these days, all clamoring for control of our inmost world, and all of them contend for the kingship of our hearts.

About ten years after my sojourn with Aragorn, I found myself besieged by the voices.

I sat in a lovely room filled with light; high windows and bookshelves clustered in the corners, a chair was pressed up in a bay window for hours of study and reading, and the sun gleamed on the old wood floor and furniture weathered by years of students before me. Everywhere I looked I saw the touches of beauty with which my mom and I had conspired to make my rented room in an old Victorian home feel like a place of refuge for me. As the digs of a soon-to-be student of English literature, it could not have been more ideal.

And I knelt on the floor in misery.

I had reached that point of inward angst where the body no longer craves comfort but only wants expression for all the emotion roiling within. A comfortable chair was an insult to the moment, an impossibility, so I knelt, knees sore and breath in the ragged tear that is the heart's panicked language of bewilderment. I had come to a crossing of ways that ambushed me. I was one week into an undergraduate degree at a respected Christian university. Classes decided, loans in place, future planned. I had sought this for months; I had worked, schemed, and submitted countless essays and even more forms to gain the very place where I now sat. I had spent a great deal of energy convincing various authorities they should admit me to this very good school, this life.

And after a week, I knew, with a conviction and finality I still find hard to explain, that it was not the place I needed to be. The story to that sense is long, but the certainty was simple. It remains in me to this day.

But I doubted myself profoundly and with good cause. I had a long history of panic attacks brought on by change, part and parcel of my mental illness. I had turned back or moved home from more than one academic venture, choices that filled me with shame yet were all I could manage in the face of crippling anxiety and depression. I knew enough to distrust my volatile emotions. I knew the panic would fade with each day that passed. So I waited. I rocked back and forth in the darkness at night. I ate and studied and went to welcome parties and did the normal, grounding things.

But something was different this time, and it wasn't a sense of peace; beneath my anxiety was a great, still quiet in which I knew that my choice for this place was wrong. Not because I was afraid, not because I was ill, but because the life I would lead here would not make me into the person I knew I had been called to become. I barely even knew what I meant by that; I wasn't sure if I had barreled through some divine warning system or let my desperate need for success blind me to everything else. But I knew, starkly and completely, that the only way forward was back.

What stopped me was imagining the twenty or so people I'd have to tell. I could hear what each of them would say, the skepticism and concern in their tones, even the anger. The voices rang already in my head so that I half agreed with them: yes, it's just illness; yes, I should push through my fear; no, I probably don't have a secret knowledge beyond everyone else; no, it's not awful here, it's just not . . . right. All those voices I'd have to answer.

A great, great quiet came suddenly upon me.

All those voices.

As I knelt on the floor I understood something vital in a flash of truth: if I let the voices drive my decision now, then they would always drive my decisions. To be human is to be always attended by a phalanx of voices telling us who to become, what to do, what to desire, and what to love.

But there is only one Voice whose words will always tell us true. I sat in the silence of that knowledge and breathed, examining the choice I was about to make and the voice leading me to it. Was it the right one, the true one?

And, *courage, dear heart*, the words from the old Narnia book came into my mind, a nudge and wink from the Person who knew me best.

It was right.

I picked up the phone and started the first of many difficult calls.

I know, because they've told me, how many people in that season thought I'd chosen wrongly. My life, from the outside, looked diminished. I went back home to the old limitations, the old daily struggles. I read my books and kept up my writing, but yes, I still yearned for a bigger world. Sometimes I ached, but I never doubted my choice.

One of the people I'd most dreaded telling of my decision was the professor who'd kindly written several letters of recommendation for me. After all his trouble on my part, I was afraid that my choice just seemed careless and ungrateful. But it had to be done.

The letter I received from him in return startled me greatly. Instead of disappointment or doubt, this kind man told me of his own difficult choice in the previous year, one that many considered foolish but he considered the only one to be made in the light of God's working in his life. Whatever processes or thoughts I'd gone through in my decision, whatever the outer reactions, he felt sure that my conclusion was not "sudden or strange from the inside."

From the inside . . . yes.

On the inside, in the realm of prayer and the kitchen table of God's presence, I knew my decision was right. My actions were not sudden or strange; they were rooted in ten years of God walking with me, shaping my imagination, bearing my grief, honing my vocation to write. If anything was strange, it was the months in which I stepped outside of that inmost place in my heart and forgot to listen to the story he was telling in my life. I can look back now and understand how much the place at that college meant in an outer way, how I yearned to catch up with my peers, why I ran toward that decision with an abandon that did not stop to consider any inmost need. Success, approval, a sense of making up for all the achievements I hadn't managed—so many outward things.

But the words from that professor grounded my resolve and made me brave. To this day, they are one of the many forces driving my sense that one of the great gifts that comes to us when we cultivate quiet, when we choose to step away from the chorus and listen to the Holy Spirit, is a capacity for conviction and courage. We need to attend in the inmost place of our hearts, where God speaks.

We need to listen and live *from the inside*.

———

Tolkien knew this; he couldn't have written his beautiful story without honing his own facility to listen from the inside.

I am a Tolkien nerd. I've read many biographies of the writer and the man. Over the years, I've found a figure not unlike Aragorn, filled in his youth with the promise of a potent creativity and academic skill, all squandered, it seemed, on the horrors and loneliness of war. But Tolkien, too, made radical choices about listening. It was on the battlefields, in the rotting, death-haunted trenches of the First World War, that Tolkien began writing a story that would bring hope to thousands. He was unique in his time, for the voices of despair were mighty.

The writers that emerged from the Great War are members of that "lost generation" we referenced earlier, those who returned from the trenches to find themselves so bewildered by the violence and death they'd witnessed that nothing made sense anymore. The old markers of faith and duty, of patriotism and hope, seemed inadequate in the face of their trauma. Many simply walked away from meaning altogether, producing magnificent and grievous works of nihilistic fiction like Fitzgerald's *The Great Gatsby*. In so many ways, Tolkien *should* have joined their number.

But Tolkien emerged from the same trenches, the same violence, to write a story about choice, about the power to be found in a fixed listening to the voices of hope. His deep Catholic faith and his sturdy friendships formed a different narrative, a story of possibility to which he attended instead of the nihilism shaping his generation. John Garth, in his excellent biography focusing on the period of Tolkien's life before and during the war, wrote about the small group of idealistic school friends who formed the "TCBS," a fellowship dedicated to "leav[ing] the world better than they had found it" by reestablishing "sanity, cleanliness, and the love of real and true beauty in everyone's breast."[4] These four friends wrote to each other from their various wartime posts to hearten each other in the long work of hope. It was one of them, Christopher, who wrote that he believed Tolkien had the power to tell a great story one day, the sort to stir the heart of the broken world.

Clearly, Tolkien listened.

Clearly, he heeded God's voice speaking him alive from the inside, even as death stalked the outer world, because on his return from the war he began to write a great story about the music God makes and the beings who listen to it well. Tolkien called his composition "The Music of the Ainur" (the *Ainu-lindalë*), a creation account of Middle Earth that would root the whole of his mythology. The *Ainulindalë* opens by introducing us to "Eru, the One" who made the Ainur (angels) as "the offspring of his thought"[5] and summoned them to participate in the making of a new and "Great Music" through which the physical world would come into being. The Ainur are called first to listen, and once they have deeply heard the song of their Creator, to add their own notes in harmony to his theme.

I find this surpassingly beautiful because I think it reflects what grows from a life of listening faith, the courage and conviction we find by rooting ourselves in quiet.

As with the Ainur, God tells the story of the world and we listen. We're called to faith mostly by responding to his voice, hearing his call above all the others in this broken world. And we need to stand awhile in silence to do this. We need to listen often, from the inside, until God's song is deeply established in our hearts. But once we know his music, we're invited to compose our lives in harmony with his, just like Tolkien's mighty angels. We're free to sing, to "adorn the work" of our Creator by lifting our voices in song. Tolkien did this in his composition of his Middle Earth and all the good stories it contains.

I did it by making a decision that looked disastrous on the outside.

But that decision meant that, by the next year, I had moved instead to Oxford. Within a week, I met the man who is now my husband and fell in love with the study of theology, two passions that now drive and define my life. My praise, my own adornment of God's theme, is to tell the story of where that voice took me, to praise the grace of a life lived from the inside. The life of quiet I've chased through the last years and have wrestled to articulate in these pages is my witness, my song. It is the harmony I'm seeking to weave with the music that shapes every moment of quiet I claim, the blessed voice that sang me alive and keeps me in life.

The voice I can hear once more every time I return to the quiet.

Prayer

O God, who knows each of us by a name spoken by no other, help us to step into the silence where we may be formed by your story. Teach us to listen and choose from the inside, to trace your love and trust your song above every other voice in this world. Let us follow you and, in the going, make our lives a harmony with yours, a place where others might catch the mighty song of their healing as your Spirit sings ever in our hearts. Through the Christ who gives us courage, Amen.

Ponder

- What voices have driven your life?
- What decisions have you made while seeing "from the inside"? Do you trust them?
- Can we have convictions apart from quiet?

12

Mara's House

Lament

The quiet I sought that day was a space to grieve.

Thomas stayed with one-year-old Lilian while I walked down to the café where my drink and name were known due to my almost daily morning attendance in that season. Usually I came with a stack of theology and about five notebooks, ready for frantic work on the graduate dissertation that was fast escaping me amidst the turmoil of our lives. Today I came only with Bible and journal and the headphones that would make the corner table by the window the cloistered space I needed. I was too restless for silence; none of my usual corners for prayer in the old Oxford churches I loved would do. Sitting in those dapple-glassed places of refuge would only remind me that what I needed to decide was whether it was right for us to leave them.

So I sat in the café window with my coffee and let the buzz of the street, the ebb and flow of humanity under the grey

spring sky, give form to the start and stop of my own stutter-
ing thoughts. But my mood did not lighten. Dread gathered
and tightened in the regions beneath my mind as I began to
understand that what I had come to hammer out was not a
decision between various options but rather my consent to
the only option available, one I could not find it in myself to
want.

For five years, Oxford had been my home, the place of an
intellectual flourishing I had long yearned to find, the city in
which I married and settled in my first little red-doored rowhouse, the place in which my first child was born. In the cobble
mazes and golden architecture and community of that place,
I knew safety, a sure sense of capability and blessing that had
been absent for many years of my life.

But my husband, after three years of training for priesthood
in the Anglican Church, was required to serve a further three-
year curacy (an internship under another priest). Our options
were limited; for various reasons, he could not do what was
usual and return to the area from which he had been sent (in
the Netherlands), so we had to consider random offers from
other churches in England. Only one had really come through,
and to me it did not seem a place we could flourish; it meant
removal to a far corner of England I barely knew, one with
no friends or connections nearby. It meant young motherhood
with no support, uncertain housing, and a church and culture that looked very different from what I knew and trusted.
I knew there would be more goodness than I could yet see, but
I also knew, viscerally, that it would be hard. I did not want
the struggle I knew would attend our lives there. I could have
wept, there in my seat in the sealed quiet of my headphones,
but I began to write instead.

And what I wrote was lament. The beat of my blood was strong in my ears, a protest that thrummed in my fingers as I penned my anguish, my sheer revolt. The quiet of that day was a stripping of any pretense I had of acceptance or calm. Quiet revealed the roil and outrage of my inmost self. When I had finished writing, I sat in a drained, ravaged silence.

Sometimes what quiet offers isn't peace but grief.

In all my long years of writing and thinking about quiet, it has always been far too easy to fall into the assumption that quiet, rightly performed, guarantees serenity. As if, should we find struggle and anger and lament in our hush, we've done it wrong. But I've learned to understand it usually means we've done it right. The gifts of quiet are nothing if not a return to what is essential, what is elemental within us: the stripped-back, barefaced truth of heart and mind. Much of that stripping does bring peace as we discover God's presence and kindness haunting our lives in countless ways we had forgotten to notice.

But the condition of all quiet in this world is that of grief.

When I picked up my Bible that day with limp, reluctant hands, feeling I had failed in my task, I turned to Psalms. In times of crisis, I must admit to an almost blinkered incapacity to find mercy in Scripture. I know it's there, but fear so shapes my sight that I become blind to God's gentleness. But the ancient, anguished poetry of the psalms has always sheltered me, given voice to my rebellion and grief. They did not fail me that day. In the regular cycle of my reading, I found myself at Psalm 31. I read listlessly until I found the words in verse 9 that gave voice to my lament: "Be gracious to me, O LORD, for I am in distress."

From that point, I read the words of the psalm as if composing them myself, until I reached David's affirmations of

God's abundant goodness, and then I slowed. I tried to mean what I read, but I failed until I stumbled into this strange and wondrous verse:

> Blessed be the LORD,
>   for he has wondrously shown his steadfast love to me
>   when I was in a besieged city.[1]

What could this mean? That David's prayer was answered, and answered well, not by removal from his uproar but with wondrous shelter in its midst? I held this idea in my mental hands, turning it over in its strangeness. Would I, then, know God's kindness in the besieged city of this unwelcome choice? Was it all right to name this decision for the hard one it was, to fully assert the distress I knew it would bring? A great hush came finally to my interior world as I understood that God did not despise the struggle revealed by my quiet but rather allowed me to understand he would be present within it. Our lives would be difficult; I knew it then and found it to be true. Those three years of curacy saw the death of Thomas's mother, the birth of two babies, demanding ministry, three moves, pneumonia, appendicitis, and a worldwide pandemic that meant we were utterly cut off from any help amidst these crises. We were indeed isolated, too far from those we loved. We were exhausted. We didn't have our family's help.

But God's kindness came to David in the very middle of deprivation and destruction, with enemies at the gates and fear in the air. God's kindness came to me countless times in that difficult place; after those three hard years I am more convinced than I have ever been before that the almighty Creator of the world involves himself in our affairs.

174

But I also know even better now that it's always amidst the siege that God's kindness arrives. We live in a world at war and will until the kingdom comes and the story of the cosmos begins again. Our pursuit of quiet will always be attended by our anguish, our wrestling, our loss. Quiet does not remove those things from us; it offers the space in which we may give voice to them so that they do not destroy us, so that the alternate voice of God's kindness may turn the besieged cities of our lives into "the rock of refuge" David found in his own wild distress.[2]

In quiet, we learn to watch and wait for God's help as it sets up camp in the very heart of our darkness.

> The weight of this sad time we must obey,
> Speak what we feel, not what we ought to say.[3]

So wrote Shakespeare in his great tragedy *King Lear*. The words end a play that is an exploration of what is most evil and most precious in this world. The innocent die and the power-hungry seem to prevail until the end, and Shakespeare "speaks" it all, obeying perhaps the weight of his own grieved heart, his own sad times, to speak the stark truth about the bitter world. But *King Lear* is also a play of redemption and renewal at the end of all things; it's about a king whose faulty sight is restored . . . if only by the death of his one faithful daughter. In *King Lear*, Shakespeare makes us witness the worst—greed and betrayal, cruelty and broken vows—but he also reveals these things for the evil they are. The truth he speaks is grieved, but it gestures to our need for something opposite to evil, an innocence Lear glimpses just before he dies.

Why is the stark honesty of lament one of the gifts of quiet?

Because it teaches us that the darkness is not our end.

Lament for the Christian is, as the great Orthodox theologian Alexander Schmemann says, a "bright sadness" because it bears at heart the belief in the reality of joy.[4] I do believe, as I said in the opening chapter of this book, that in quiet we stand in the light of the new heavens and the new earth. I believe that quiet allows us to return to the presence of our Maker, he who dwells out of time in unchangeable peace, but we walk our way home to him by the confession of our grief. We walk home to him on the highway of our sorrow and find him already present, the one who gives us strength to carry on. Our lament may be the only road by which we may walk into the presence of the only Help who can answer our grief.

George MacDonald, a Scottish writer and poet beloved by C. S. Lewis, wrote a story about this kind of holy grief. His books glimmer with all sorts of insight and mystery, but just after the death of his beloved daughter, in the evening of his life, he wrote a novel called *Lilith*. Those near him say he was so grief-stricken in that season he could barely speak. He closed himself in his study, and the book came to him like fire.

Lilith is a strange book, no bones about it. It is a ramble through a landscape of guilt and grief, forgiveness and redemption, all embodied in fantastical forms, in desert places and skeletons, in evil queens and gentle children. It's the story of a man who enters an alternate reality and meets Adam and Eve, now redeemed and restored, and is set upon a journey through their land by which he, too, must learn how to die to all that he has been so that he may finally live. He begins with great suspicion, not understanding how the forces of sorrow and confession, of trust in a self greater than his own, of forgiveness, might cleanse and heal him utterly.

But all pilgrims in that country must pass through Mara's house, and our hero is no exception. Mara is the child of Adam and Eve, born from their grief and repentance. Her sorrow is holy. She lives in the desert, and every traveler eventually comes to her great, silent house. Each pilgrim must eat her bread and drink her cold, cold water. Her face is veiled, and at first our hero finds this suspicious; he dreads what he might find beneath this covering.

Mara is MacDonald's embodiment of the grace to be found in lament. In the desert quiet of loss, when we dwell in the house of sorrow, we expect to find only a slow disintegration. But in God's hands, our grief becomes the road to healing, our lament becomes the companion leading us to the source of our lost joy. In the book, when each traveler finally sees Mara's face unveiled, what he or she finds is a radiance of compassion. Her house shelters all who search for life amidst the storm, and her food gives the strength required to travel through death to the love that waits on the other side.

I think that sometimes quiet comes to us as Mara's house.

Quiet is the stark, silent refuge our grieved hearts crave, the space in which sorrow becomes the means of hope. Mara's bread makes us honest. Her drink is the kind of tonic that cleanses the mind of inhibition or resentment, that freshens our eyes so we may see and speak our need. The silence of her house is the great, great hush that comes as we watch for the dawn.

Alfred Delp, a Jesuit priest in Germany who was imprisoned and sentenced to death by the Nazis, wrote one of the most stirring passages of hope I have ever read. He, too, sat in Mara's house, isolated, awaiting his trial in a Nazi jail cell. But in that darkness he spoke his grief and need, and what he found himself writing about was Advent, that season in which we speak our longing from the darkness even as we cry aloud for the light.

> Space is still filled with the noise of destruction and annihilation, the shouts of self-assurance and arrogance, the weeping of despair and helplessness. But round about the horizon the eternal realities stand silent in their age-old longing. There shines on them already the first mild light of the radiant fulfillment to come. From afar sound the first notes as of pipes and voices, not yet discernible as a song or melody. It is all far off still, and only just announced and foretold. But it is happening, today.[5]

I believe a life shaped by quiet allows us to catch the echo of "the first notes" of God's arrival, even in the very heart of our sadness.

Six months after my anguished day of journaling in Oxford, I stood in an old Danish church.

My breath was short as I walked, the tug and tumble of a coming baby shoving up against my ribs. I sat in one of the straight-backed pews, the wood smoothed dark and sheeny by countless worshipers. Late, wintered light slanted through the high windows, brittle and clear. My toddler ran into all the corners as I allowed myself the simple grace of slow breaths and tried to catch at the long, long quiet our coming had disturbed. Then I heard her familiar cry of "Dat," her way of asking what something was, a cry she would not cease until one of her parents noticed and answered. I lumbered up, knowing my husband was just coming in with the stroller.

She was pointing to a ship, a perfect little model of a ship with full sails suspended from the church ceiling. "Ship," I said, but turned to my half-Danish husband to ask what this meant. Such ships, he said, were common in Danish churches. They reminded the faithful that the church was a kind of holy ship, bearing the people of God through the high seas of a stormy world, right to the shores of the new world to come. To enter the quiet refuge of a church was, in a sense, to know oneself cradled and safe whatever storm might rage.

Thomas took our little one to explore the odd corners, and I sat down again to gaze at that ship and think about refuge. We'd settled now in our new home. Six months of working to make our odd little house (with its grudging landlord) feel homey had at least left us with a sense of our own space and rooting. I still couldn't think of Oxford and our friendships there without a stomach-drop of loss, and the growth of community was slow. The frantic days that led up to our move had abruptly sunk into the great quiet of this different life. Most of my days were slow now after years of social and academic intensity. At first I'd found it oppressive, this pervasive absence of anything to run for or do.

But the child in my belly had helped to calm me. Time is nothing but slow in pregnancy. There's a kind of contraction of the world that comes as the body calls in all its resources to meet the demands of a new, small being. Amidst it I found myself wooed by a great quiet, one that surprised me with its grace. I felt it as an invitation in the cool mornings when I woke to walls and skies I did not recognize. I felt it as the urge to sink myself into the wide, lonely hush as if into a healing pool of water. The edges of our days blurred, our movements slowed, the silence grew. I felt myself afloat in a different kind

179

of world as the cadence of my hours drew down to the rounds of sleeping and waking, gulls singing in the dawn, to slow hours in the park or garden, or on the couch with a pile of picture books. Sometimes I wasn't sure where it was all leading me, who I would become on the other side of the Oxford years and in this new, vast space of hush.

But there, with that little ship suspended as a sign above my head, I remembered the verse that had come in the spring: "He has made marvelous His lovingkindness to me in a besieged city."[6] I, too, was afloat in a little ship of kindness, a vessel of quiet that kept me safe. Not drifting but steered through all the roiling of my sadness, all the uproar of the new and the unsurety of what lurked over our horizons. The great lament of my leaving had led me into the safety of this kindness, this marvelous quiet in which I knew myself sheltered and safe in the hands of God, steered by his generous love toward goodness I had not yet even imagined.

As I am now. As I will ever be.

Quiet in this world; perhaps it is most often the vessel that bears us out of darkness and into hope.

Prayer

O God, teach us to speak our sorrow. Teach us the grace of saying the word that cannot be held inside, the grief that cannot be bounded by our own frail hearts but only by your world-making hands. Help us to seek the quiet place of your presence and find it the space where a marvelous kindness encircles our lives. Teach us to grieve, teach us to yearn, and let these be the friends who lead us to hope.

May we, with all your people, sail safely through the wild waters of this world until we reach the shores where sorrow is ended and joy dawns like the morning, through Jesus, the Captain and Keeper of our souls, Amen.

Ponder

- Set aside a time of quiet to articulate what grieves you. Speak what you feel . . . not what you ought to say.
- How, for you, might lament be a way that leads to hope?
- When have you sojourned in Mara's house, and what did you find in those seasons?

Acknowledgments

The pursuit of quiet and the writing of a book are both ostensibly interior, individual tasks, but both are works that require the kindness, patience, and encouragement of others if they are ever to flourish. In closing this book, I find myself mightily grateful to those who have allowed me the gracious space to reclaim quiet and wrestle out these words.

I am so grateful to my husband, Thomas, for the way he has protected and provided for my writing life. From the earliest days of our marriage, he has made purposeful space for me to be creatively alone, to pray, and to write. This book (and any other I've written in the past years) would not exist without his encouragement, his generous gift of time, and the love that continues to make me starry-eyed.

Fr. Mark Stafford has been a counselor, spiritual director, and friend of rare insight and generosity. I am so grateful for our many conversations, for the shelter and challenge I have found in his words.

Rev. Dr. Liz Hoare has been a kindred-spirit companion and mentor in life and in the pursuit of quiet since my first years at Oxford. It is an ongoing delight to exchange ideas, books, and thoughts about the interior life with her. I am so grateful for her influence and friendship.

I will be grateful all my days for my parents, Clay and Sally Clarkson, who understood the gift of a childhood framed by imagination, holy boredom, good words, and space to explore. I bear wide spaces within my soul because of their generosity and courage in shaping my earliest days.

My agent, Alex Field, is the best of agents: capable, insightful, and warm. I'm so grateful for his guidance and friendship in bringing these books to life.

My publisher, Rebekah Von Lintel, was extremely gracious in allowing me several extensions of writing time to finish this book, a decision that brought the gift of quiet to my own life in a healing way.

My editor, Jamie Chavez, was a delight to work with. She made the editing process a lively conversation between friends, and I am grateful for her fun and insight in this task. Lindsey Spoolstra also gave kind attention to the smallest details of this book, making words flow and paragraphs sing.

Brianna DeWitt is, as she has been before, a wondrous weaver of many important particulars, the answerer of many questions, and organizer of literary endeavors. I'm grateful for her care and excellence.

Finally, I'm so thankful for my children, these gracious little souls who daily teach me to walk the paths of wonder, to live the great adventure of quiet. I could not ask for better companions.

Notes

Chapter 1 Kitchen Table in My Heart

1. Brother Lawrence, *Writings and Conversations on the Practice of the Presence of God*, critical edition, edited by Conrad De Meester, translated by Salvatore Sciurba (Washington, DC: ICS Publications, 1993), 73.

2. From a traditional Celtic prayer titled "The Lightener of the Stars," in *Carmina Gadelica*, vol. 1, edited by Alexander Carmichael (Edinburgh: T. and A. Constable, 1900), https://sacred-texts.com/neu/celt/cg1/cg1019.htm#page_45.

3. St. Athanasius the Great of Alexandria, *On the Incarnation*, translated by John Behr (Yonkers, NY: St. Vladimir's Seminary Press, 2011), 173.

Chapter 2 Native Ground

1. Denise Levertov, "Psalm Fragments (Schnittke String Trio)," in *The Collected Poems of Denise Levertov* (New York: New Directions, 2013).

2. Isaiah 43:1.

Chapter 3 Trust amidst Apocalypse

1. John 14:27.

2. David Bentley Hart, *The Beauty of the Infinite: The Aesthetics of Christian Truth* (Grand Rapids: Eerdmans, 2004), 127.

3. Hart, *Beauty of the Infinite*, 127.

4. "H7965: šālôm," Strong's Concordance, accessed January 29, 2024, https://www.blueletterbible.org/lexicon/h7965/niv/wlc/0-1/.

Chapter 4 Lover's Quest

1. Elizabeth Barrett Browning, "Aurora Leigh," in *The Oxford Book of English Mystical Verse*, edited by D. H. S. Nicholson and A. H. E. Lee (Oxford: Clarendon Press, 1917), 146.

2. Charles Taylor, *A Secular Age* (Cambridge: Harvard University Press, 2007).

3. C. S. Lewis, *The Weight of Glory: And Other Addresses* (New York: HarperOne, 2001), 29.

4. C. S. Lewis, *Surprised by Joy: The Shape of My Early Life* (New York: Harcourt, Brace & World, 1955); J. R. R. Tolkien, *Tree and Leaf* (London: HarperCollins UK, 2012), 69.

5. Lisel Mueller, "Joy," in *Alive Together: New and Selected Poems* (Baton Rouge: Louisiana State University Press, 1996), 199.

6. Willa Cather, *The Song of the Lark* (New York: Barnes & Noble, 2008), 139.

7. Taylor, *Secular Age*, 5.

8. "H6960: *qāvâ*," Strong's Concordance, accessed January 30, 2024, https://www.blueletterbible.org/lexicon/h6960/nasb20/wlc/0-1/.

9. Luke 13:34.

10. Gerard Manley Hopkins, "God's Grandeur," *Poems and Prose* (New York: Penguin Classics, 1953), 27.

Chapter 5 Ox-Cart Man

1. Donald Hall, *Ox-Cart Man*, illustrated by Barbara Cooney (New York: Viking, 1979).

2. Tobias Wolff, *Old School* (London: Bloomsbury Publishing, 2005), 53.

3. Hans Urs von Balthasar, *Theo-Drama IV: The Action* (San Francisco: Ignatius Press, 1994), 149.

4. Balthasar, *Theo-Drama IV*, 151.

5. Donald Hall, "Summer Kitchen," in *White Apples and the Taste of Stone: Selected Poems, 1946–2006* (Boston: Mariner Books, 2007), 375.

Chapter 6 Words Make Worlds

1. The italicized lines of prayer in this chapter are all drawn from either the liturgies in the Anglican Book of Common Prayer (Evening Prayer and Morning Prayer) or the Common Worship form of Compline in traditional language.

2. From the catechism in the 1662 Book of Common Prayer.

3. Hans Boersma, *Heavenly Participation: The Weaving of a Sacramental Tapestry* (Grand Rapids: Eerdmans, 2011), 127.

Chapter 7 Color of Wonder

1. Elizabeth Goudge, *The Scent of Water* (London: Hodder & Stoughton, 1963), 93.

2. Robert Louis Stevenson, "The Celestial Surgeon," in *A Child's Garden of Verses and Underwoods* (New York: Current Literature Publishing, 1906), 54.

3. Brother Lawrence, *The Practice of the Presence of God*, translated by Joseph de Beaufort (Mount Vernon, NY: Peter Pauper Press, 1963), 48.

4. Reginald Heber, "Brightest and Best of the Sons of the Morning" (1811), public domain.

Chapter 8 Halcyon Day

1. Edna St. Vincent Millay, "Afternoon on a Hill," Poets.org, accessed February 22, 2024, https://poets.org/poem/afternoon-hill.

2. Alexander Schmemann, *For the Life of the World* (Crestwood, NY: SVS Press, 2004), 14.

3. New Advent Encyclopedia, s.v. "recollection," accessed January 31, 2024, https://www.newadvent.org/cathen/12676b.htm.

4. Abraham Joshua Heschel, *The Sabbath* (New York: Farrar, Straus and Giroux, repr. 2004), 74.

5. Genesis 3:19.

Chapter 9 Becoming Small

1. Luke 16:10.

2. John 7:17.

3. Denise Levertov, "Annunciation," in *The Collected Poems of Denise Levertov* (New York: New Directions, 2013), 838.

4. Levertov, "Annunciation," 836.

5. Zechariah 4:10.

6. Marilynne Robinson, *Lila* (London: Virago Press, 2014), 135.

Chapter 10 Wise Woman's Cottage

1. "H3824: *lēḇāḇ*," Strong's Concordance, accessed February 1, 2024, https://www.blueletterbible.org/lexicon/h3824/nasb95/wlc/0-1/.

2. Matthew 5:8.

3. C. S. Lewis, *Surprised by Joy* (London: Harper Collins, 2002), 17.

4. J. R. R. Tolkien, "Mythopoeia," in *Tree and Leaf; Mythopoeia; The Homecoming of Beorhtnoth Beorhthelm's Son* (London: Harper, 2001).

5. Hebrews 11:1.

6. C. S. Lewis, "Meditation in a Toolshed," in *God in the Dock* (Grand Rapids: Eerdmans, 1998), 212–15.

7. Margaret Hodges, *Saint George and the Dragon*, illustrated by Trina Schart Hyman (Boston: Little, Brown and Co., 1984).

8. G. K. Chesterton, "The Red Angel," in *Tremendous Trifles* (Project Gutenberg, 2005), accessed February 22, 2024, https://www.gutenberg.org/cache/epub/8092/pg8092-images.html.

Chapter 11 Seeing from the Inside

1. J. R. R. Tolkien, *The Lord of the Rings: Deluxe Illustrated Edition*, illustrated by Alan Lee (New York: Houghton Mifflin, 1991), 894.

2. John 10:27.

3. 1 Kings 19:12.

4. John Garth, *Tolkien and the Great War: The Threshold of Middle-Earth* (London: HarperCollins, 2011), 105.

5. J. R. R. Tolkien, *The Silmarillion* (London: HarperCollins, 1998), 15.

Chapter 12 Mara's House

1. Psalm 31:21 ESV.

2. Psalm 31:2 ESV.

3. William Shakespeare, *King Lear* 5.3.323–24.

4. Alexander Schmemann, *Great Lent: Journey to Pascha* (Crestwood, NY: St. Vladimir's Seminary Press, 1969), 36.

5. Alfred Delp, "The Shaking Reality of Advent," in *Watch for the Light: Readings for Advent and Christmas* (Walden, NY: Plough Publishing House, 2001), 95.

6. Psalm 31:21.

Sarah Clarkson is a writer and speaker exploring the intersection of beauty, suffering, and imagination. She studied theology at Wycliffe Hall, Oxford (BTh, MSt) with research focused on the role of beauty in theodicy. She is the author of seven books, including *This Beautiful Truth: How God's Goodness Breaks into Our Darkness*. She lives in an Oxford vicarage with her husband, Thomas, and their four children, and writes regularly about books, beauty, and theology in her newsletter and in various publications like *Plough*, *Comment* magazine, and others. You can join her for regular live poetry readings on her Instagram @SarahWanders, join her literary fellowship on Patreon (Patreon .com/SarahClarkson), or follow her work and sign up for her newsletter at SarahClarkson.com.

Connect with Sarah:

SarahClarkson.com
Facebook: @SarahEClarkson
Instagram: @SarahWanders
X: @ThoroughlyAlive
Patreon: Sarah Clarkson
Substack: Beautiful Truths with Sarah Clarkson